# SAN DIEGO
## —YESTERDAY—

*Richard W. Crawford*

THE
History
PRESS

Published by The History Press
Charleston, SC 29403
www.historypress.net

Copyright © 2013 by Richard W. Crawford
All rights reserved

*Cover images*: Images on top of front and bottom of back from Special Collections, San
Diego Public Library.

First published 2013

ISBN 9781540208279

Library of Congress CIP data applied for.

# CONTENTS

# PREFACE

San Diego is a city with an extraordinary history. Founded by Spanish missionaries in 1769, this "birthplace of California" has grown from an impoverished frontier seaport to become the eighth-largest city in America. In the nearly two and a half centuries in between, the region has seen bitter war and restless peace, civic pride and municipal scandal, gifted leaders and bizarre personalities. Many of the more fascinating stories from this history are recounted here in *San Diego Yesterday*.

Like a predecessor volume—*The Way We Were in San Diego*—the articles here first appeared in a weekly newspaper column for the *San Diego Union-Tribune*. They are presented here in their original length, often with added historical photographs. Many individuals and institutions have generously provided reference help and historical images for this volume. I would like to thank the Naval Historical Foundation; Robert Ray, Special Collections, San Diego State University Library; Ronald W. Evans, San Diego State University; Steve Willard and Tom Giaquinto, San Diego Police Museum; Steven Coy, Special Collections, University of California–San Diego; Bruce Semelsberger, Pacific Southwest Railway Museum; Carol Myers and Natalie Fiocre, San Diego History Center; Sarah Hartwell, Rauner Special Collections, Dartmouth College; Robert Finch, San Diego Electric Railway Association; Lisa Glandt, Vancouver Maritime Museum; and Therese Garcia, Portuguese Historical Center. Individuals who have kindly provided from their own collections include Jeff Madruga, Lucile Madruga and Bob and Tennie Bee Hall. I am sincerely grateful to you all.

# PART I

# A FRONTIER PORT BECOMES A CITY

## THE HORTON HOUSE

*The great need of this town is about to be supplied by A.E. Horton, Esq.,
who will immediately erect, on the northwest corner of Fourth and D Streets, a
palatial brick edifice, for hotel purposes. It is to contain a hundred rooms and to
be fitted up with elegant furniture and all modern improvements.*
    —San Diego Bulletin, *December 18, 1869*

San Diego in 1869 was on the verge of a boom. A railroad connection to the
east, which would make San Diego the terminus of the first transcontinental
railroad, seemed likely. Anticipating the link, real estate sales boomed. The
*Bulletin* declared, "From a place of no importance, the home of a squirrel a
few months back, we now have a city of three thousand inhabitants."

Only two years earlier, a businessman from San Francisco, Alonzo
Erastus Horton, had started it all by buying San Diego pueblo land near
the port—not far from the failed town site of William H. Davis, whose
1850s venture was already known as "Davis' Folly." Horton succeeded by
selling off lots of "Horton's Addition" at bargain prices to attract settlers
and businesses. For many investors, the impending arrival of the railroad
clinched the deal.

On New Year's Day 1870, Horton broke ground for a first-class hotel
that would be the centerpiece of the rising city. A shipload of rough lumber

was "promiscuously dumped" around a brush-covered site on D Street, and "nearly all" the carpenters and bricklayers in town set to work. Horton's brother-in-law, W.W. Bowers, supervised the construction of the hotel, working from a crude sketch of San Francisco's famed Russ House as a model. The two-and-a-half-story, one-hundred-room hotel was finished in only nine months at the cost of $150,000.

The Horton House opened on October 10, 1870, to rave public reviews. Calling itself "the largest and finest hotel in California south of San Francisco," it featured gas lighting and rich carpeting throughout the building, rooms with steam heaters and marble washstands filled with "pure soft water" conveyed by pipes (from a well) and bathrooms running both hot and cold water. Perhaps the

Alonzo Erastus Horton, builder of the Horton House. *Special Collections, San Diego Public Library.*

hotel's proudest achievement was "an electrical bell apparatus, with wires," which ran to the office from every room.

The hotel soon operated at capacity and brought new business to San Diego. Hotel guests paid $2.50 for a room, meals included. The *San Diego Union* noted that "Horton has met the great need of our young city. He did it by building and keeping a first class hotel...the Horton House has done more for San Diego than all other improvements combined."

Horton kept the ownership of the hotel for several years, but only with difficulty. In 1873, the railroad syndicate that had promised a terminus in San Diego collapsed. San Diego's boom faltered, and Horton found himself in financial trouble. He leased the Horton House and looked, unsuccessfully, for a buyer of the hotel. He also borrowed money, using his hotel as collateral. When Horton defaulted on a loan from a local businessman, he almost lost the property.

San Diego's Horton House, the "finest hotel in California south of San Francisco," opened in October 1870. *Special Collections, San Diego Public Library.*

In *M.S. Patrick v. A.E. Horton*, it was alleged that $4,107 was owed to Mr. Patrick. To satisfy the debt, the district court issued a writ of attachment that demanded that Horton surrender all the furnishings of the hotel. Horton survived the crisis, but the court case file, which contained a room-by-room inventory of the Horton House, provided lavish evidence of the "best style" for which the hotel was known.

The attachment papers listed the contents of every room: hotel office, sleeping rooms, bar, library, billiard room and dining room. The most minimal bedroom contained a bedstead with sheets, pillows and blankets, as well as towel racks, chamber pot, spittoon and chair. More sumptuous quarters added loungers and rocking chairs. Some rooms boasted pianos, marble center tables and oil paintings on walls. The hotel bar was well stocked with nearly one hundred varieties of liquor and several thousand cigars.

For several more years, Horton leased out the hotel while he struggled with mortgage payments, but foreclosure loomed. Finally, in August 1881, the *Union* politely reported, "We take pleasure in announcing that the Horton House has passed into the hands of W.E. Hadley, who took charge yesterday evening."

William Hadley would run the Horton House for the next two decades, occasionally making renovations and small additions. In March 1886, the hotel boasted the "first private electric light in the city." As the hotel's premier status was gradually eclipsed by newer hostelries, Hadley promoted his "moderate" prices with "special rates to families."

On August 12, 1895, a headline in the *San Diego Union* blared, "Horton House Is Sold." The buyer was the family of U.S. Grant Jr., who paid $52,251 for the property. "It is understood," the newspaper reported, that Grant will eventually build "a grand hotel building" on the site of the Horton House.

Years of rumors followed about a possible new hotel. In 1903, the *Union* reported that architects Hebbard and Gill had drawn preliminary plans for the site. The plans were never used. More time would pass before U.S. Grant Jr. decided to tear down the Horton House and build a new hotel as a monument to his father, President Grant.

On July 12, 1905, a large crowd watched as Alonzo Horton, age ninety-one, ceremoniously removed a brick from the hotel he had built thirty-five year earlier. Turning to the crowd, Horton said that it was his wish that the brick be used "in the principal wall of the new structure."

Construction of the new hotel, designed by Harrison Albright, began but then stopped, delayed by the San Francisco earthquake and funding difficulties. Five more years would go by before the U.S. Grant Hotel officially opened on October 15, 1910.

# CABLE CARS IN SAN DIEGO

*One of the great needs of San Diego for some time past has been a system of cable street railroads. This improved method of covering long distances in cities has become very popular in all of the metropolises of the country, and it has been one great improvement in which San Diego was deficient.*
–San Diego Union, *June 9, 1889*

Urban public transportation in the late 1800s meant streetcars—not the "time-honored horse car" or experimental electric lines but "grip cars," pulled smoothly through city streets by a continuous iron cable. San Francisco mastered the cable technology in the 1870s. Other growing West Coast cities followed: Seattle, Portland, Oakland and Los Angeles.

In the summer of 1889, San Diegans eagerly waited for the construction of their own modern cable car railway. Investors, led by bankers D.D. Dare and J.W. Collins, pooled their money for startup costs. "Within one year," prophesied the *Union*, streetcars would cover "the main business portion of the city, passing by some of the finest suburban residences here, and giving direct and easy communication with the heart of the city...The citizen residing on University Heights will be whirled down to his place of business by a commodious car, propelled by a steam cable."

The San Diego Cable Railway Company was incorporated in July 1889. Dare and Collins were elected president and treasurer, respectively. City Alderman John C. Fisher was vice-president and general manager. The chief engineer, tasked with building the railway, was Frank Van Vleck, who had gained experience working on the Los Angeles Cable Railroad.

Van Vleck planned a five-mile route that ran from the foot of Sixth Street to C, then up the hill on Fourth Street to University Avenue, where it turned east for several blocks before continuing north on what became Park Boulevard and Adams Avenue, ending at the "Bluffs" over Mission Valley. The route was designed to take advantage of potential real estate sales in the barren, undeveloped stretches along upper Sixth and the heights above Mission Valley.

"Dirt flew" in August when a crew of two hundred men began excavating the four-foot-wide trench that would hold the tracks and cable. The steel rails, weighing thirty pounds per yard, rested on an iron frame, or "yoke," set in concrete. The 1⅛-inch, iron-strand cable ran through an underground conduit centered between the tracks. As the line neared completion, a team of twenty horses pulled fifty thousand feet of cable through the conduit.

To save money, the line was built as a single-track, meaning cable cars moved north and south on the same rails. Sidings allowed cars to pass in opposite directions, and turntables at the ends of the line let the cars turn around. A power plant at Fourth and Spruce generated the steam to turn massive winding wheels for pulling the cable.

After "innumerable and vexatious delays," the railway opened on June 7, 1890. A day of congratulatory speeches and festivities heralded the inauguration. Governor Robert Waterman and other dignitaries took rides in streetcars decorated with flags and flowers. Renowned horticulturist Kate Sessions was said to be the first paying passenger.

The streetcar line ran with twelve "combination" cars—one half closed and the other open—similar to San Francisco's Powell Street cable cars. San Diego's "gorgeous palaces on wheels"—built in Stockton and shipped to San Diego—boasted stained-glass clerestory windows, coal-oil lighting and surfaces of nickel-plate and hardwood. A novel innovation was electric stop-bells powered by batteries beneath the seats. Cars were named—not

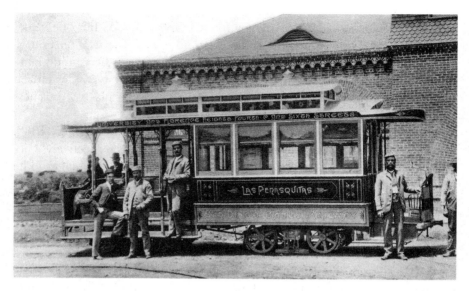

San Diego's "gorgeous palaces on wheels" were named to highlight San Diego communities, such as "Las Penasquitas." *San Diego Electric Railway Association.*

The cable car barn at Fourth and Spruce Streets. *Southwest Railway Library, Pacific Southwest Railway Museum.*

numbered—to highlight San Diego communities: "El Escondido," "El Cajon," "La Jolla," "Point Loma" and "San Ysidora."

The attendants wore gray uniforms and caps, with gold buttons for the conductors and silver for the grip men. For pay of eighteen cents per hour, they alternated a "short day" of 5:30 a.m. to 3:15 p.m. with a "long day" of 5:30 a.m. to 11:00 p.m., with one hour off for lunch. The crews were responsible for buying their own uniforms (about twenty dollars) and cleaning their own streetcars.

The cable cars were popular, particularly on weekends. For a fare of one nickel, riders traveled at eight to ten miles per hour from downtown to uptown in University Heights in as little as ten minutes. Trailers were sometimes attached to the cars to accommodate large crowds. A popular attraction for families was the Bluffs on the northern end of the line. Later known as Mission Cliff Gardens, the park featured six acres of terraced walks and gardens on the canyon rim overlooking Mission Valley. There were band concerts, dances and traveling shows from a pavilion stage.

But for all its popularity, the system lost money for the Cable Railway Company. Installation of the line had been costly, and ongoing operating costs strained the cash flow. Brakes needed servicing weekly, and the cable grips had to be replaced every three weeks. The company was also forced to pay for expensive street paving in roadways that were only dirt when the tracks were laid.

A banking scandal precipitated the end. In November 1891, the California National Bank closed its doors. The bank's president, J.W. Collins, was arrested for embezzlement, while D.D. Dare fled to Europe. The two men had been principal backers of the cable railway, and with their bank gone, the company went into receivership.

For the next several months, court-appointed receivers managed the railway, which limped along, running fewer cars to save money. A broken cable closed a portion of the line in late summer. New cable was ordered, but with no money to install it, the company chose to shut down forever on October 15, 1892.

# THE CARNEGIE LIBRARY

*If the city were to pledge itself to maintain a free public library from taxes,
say to the extent of the amount you name, of between five and six thousand
dollars a year, and provide a site, I shall be glad to give you $50,000 to
erect a suitable library building.*

*—Andrew Carnegie, July 7, 1899*

Between 1883 and 1929, the industrialist turned philanthropist Andrew
Carnegie funded construction of 1,689 libraries in the United States. San
Diego had the honor of being the first Carnegie library in California.

Since its founding in 1882, the San Diego Public Library struggled to find
adequate funding and a permanent home. Rented floors in a bank building
at Fifth and G Streets served the book collection for its first decade. Cost-
cutting forced a move in 1893 to rooms in the St. James Building at Seventh
and F Streets. Another move came in 1898 to the fifth floor of the Keating
Building at Fifth and F. With only meager financial support from the city,
a permanent home for the library seemed unlikely.

Library supporters were not
discouraged. The Wednesday Club,
an "artistic and literary culture"
club of San Diego women, adopted
the library as its special project.
Led by Lydia Knapp Horton, the
wife of San Diego founder Alonzo
Horton, the women began a library
building fund.

Lydia Knapp Horton lobbied
philanthropist Andrew Carnegie for
funding to build San Diego's first library
building. *Special Collections, San Diego
Public Library.*

In October 1897, Lydia Horton wrote to Andrew Carnegie requesting pictures of library buildings he had sponsored. The philanthropist mailed a set of prints, which the Wednesday Club exhibited as a fundraiser. Mrs. Horton continued the correspondence, telling Carnegie in May 1899 that "the library needs of this place are very apparent...we feel more than ever the need of permanent quarters." Carnegie responded with the offer of $50,000 to build "a suitable library building."

Amid the excitement over Carnegie's generous offer, the project immediately bogged down in debate over where to locate the new building. Several different downtown sites were promoted for the honor. The size of the property was also questioned; businessman George W. Marston argued strongly for a whole block and warned that "the city will regret for all time its error if it should let this opportunity pass without obtaining the full square of land for the library."

After several months of public acrimony, a half-block tract of land was purchased at Eighth and E Streets for $17,000. The city paid only $9,000, with the remainder coming from private donations, including $1,000 from George Marston and $500 from the Wednesday Club.

Bids for the construction of the library were solicited in a national competition. The request for proposals called for a building "as nearly fireproof as possible," using granite or brick construction. All rooms were to receive as much natural light as possible, "as all Californians recognize the necessity of sunny rooms." The successful architects would receive 5 percent of the building budget as full compensation for their plans and specifications.

The design competition was won by Ackerman and Ross. The New York architectural firm had recently designed a Carnegie library in Washington, D.C. The San Diego architectural firm Hebbard and Gill was subcontracted by Ackerman and Ross as construction superintendents.

Construction for the library began in December 1900. Sixteen months later, on April 23, 1902, the library opened. The completed building was a beautiful, Classical Revival–style structure, built of brick and covered with white cement, giving a marble appearance to the exterior. The library was fronted by a grass lawn, with landscaping designed by horticulturist Kate Sessions and funded by George Marston.

Library historian Theodore Koch (*A Book of Carnegie Libraries*, 1917) described the library's interior:

> *The delivery room* [circulation desk] *occupies the center of the first floor; opening from this, on the one side, are a children's room and a women's*

San Diego's Carnegie library opened at Eighth and E Streets in April 1902. *Special Collections, San Diego Public Library.*

The men's reading room in the Carnegie library. In the early 1900s, the sexes were segregated in most public libraries. *Special Collections, San Diego Public Library.*

*magazine room; on the other a men's magazine room and a reference room. Behind the delivery room are the librarian's and catalogers' rooms, back of which are the stacks. The second story contains an art gallery, a lecture room with seating capacity of 100, a museum, trustees' room, and two small rooms for special study. The light green tint of the walls throughout the building blends harmoniously with the color of the oak furniture.*

With furnishings, the building had ultimately cost $60,000. The steel book stacks alone cost nearly $10,000. Fortunately, the Carnegie foundation agreed to increase its gift to cover the added costs, with the condition that the City of San Diego agree to support the library with at least $6,000 per year.

The new library reflected both new and old attitudes of public librarianship. Separate reading rooms for men and women were normal practice for the day. A central delivery desk for requested books was also a time-honored practice. But the library's interest in service for children—apparent in the large children's room—was quite modern. More revolutionary still was a willingness to allow patrons into the library stacks to choose books themselves, without a librarian's help. In 1902, the San Diego Public Library was among the first public libraries to offer "open stacks."

The size of the Carnegie building, designed for a city population of only 17,700 in 1900, seemed to shrink rapidly in just a few years. By 1910, the San Diego population had more than doubled in size, and the library had begun to suffer from crowding. In a few more years, shelving covered every available wall surface. Short-term relief came from moving several departments to rented spaces in nearby buildings. Remodeling the Carnegie in 1930 added more floor space, and the addition of new branch libraries took some pressure off.

However, the need for a larger library was clear. After failed bond measures in 1923 and 1937, the voters finally approved $2 million in bonds in 1949 to build a new main library and improve the growing branch library system. Three years later, the library moved into temporary quarters in an old exposition building in Balboa Park. The venerable Carnegie library, at age fifty, was demolished. The new Central Library, designed for a city population of less than 350,000, was built on the same site and dedicated on June 27, 1954.

# THE SAN DIEGO BATHS

*Salvation for the great unwashed is now offered in the waters of the Tropical Natatorium at the foot of D Street. This institution is thrown open to the public today. No pains have been spared for the comfort of the people.*
—San Diego Union, *November 27, 1886*

There was a time in America when the standard for personal cleanliness was a weekly bath. The "great unwashed" often found that Saturday night soak in commercial bathhouses, such as the esteemed Tropical Natatorium, where bathers could indulge in warm, saltwater dips along the seashore. During San Diego's population "boom of the eighties," nearly a dozen bathhouses dotted the city's waterfront.

San Diego's first recorded bathhouse, Cotterel & White, opened in 1869 near Horton's Wharf at the foot of Fifth Street. The first facility was a simple affair: a wire netting suspended alongside a barge formed a "swimming bath," twelve by thirty feet. The barge provided dressing rooms and rental bathing suits.

Later bathhouses were fashioned from corrals of wooden stakes, pounded into the mud of the bay. The corrals sheltered the bathers from vagaries of the surf and also offered protection against the notorious stingrays of San Diego bay. The baths were open seasonally, usually from May until October.

Captain John Heerandner's Caroline Bath House, at the foot of Sixth Street, was a popular success in the early 1880s. Heerandner drew evening crowds for his moonlight concerts featuring the San Diego Brass Band. The concerts were free. Bathers paid the usual fifteen cents. Heerandner also boasted a swimming coach from Sidney, Australia, who gave "instructions and exhibitions of his skill to all who so desire."

Heerandner's chief competitor was W.W. Collier, operating from the steamship wharf at the foot of Fifth Street. Collier claimed that his "accommodations for lady bathers [were] especially good" and featured large, floating tanks. The mornings were reserved for the women, as the *Union* announced: "Mrs. Collier gives her personal attention to lady bathers, and those who wish to learn to swim will have an excellent opportunity these warm sunny forenoons."

Mrs. Collier's lady bathers had a scare one day when their floating tanks nearly met disaster. "The cable at the steamship wharf bathhouse broke yesterday," announced the *Union*. "The great tubs were about to go to sea while several ladies were indulging in the invigorating exercise of a swim. The cable was soon repaired, however, and the danger averted."

Los Banos, at Broadway and Kettner Boulevard, was an architectural showcase designed by architects William S. Hebbard and Irving J. Gill. *Special Collections, San Diego Public Library.*

The Tropical Natatorium would easily eclipse the seasonal bathing corrals and floating tubs of Heerandner and Collier when it opened in November 1886 at the foot of D Street (today's Broadway). Groundbreaking, for San Diego, was the two-hundred- by one-hundred-foot lined swimming bath, open to the bay. Seawater flowed through gates that opened and closed automatically with the tide. The facility boasted of electric lighting, steam-heated tub baths, Turkish steam rooms and an amphitheater. The giant pool featured "swings, slides, spring-boards and other things dear to the heart of the amateur athlete."

In August 1897, the ultimate San Diego bath experience opened one block away from the Tropical Natatorium across the street from the Santa Fe depot. Los Banos was an architectural showcase. Built by Graham E. Babcock, the son of Coronado developer Elisha S. Babcock, the bathhouse was a red-tiled, Neo Moorish–style structure designed by the architects William S. Hebbard and Irving J. Gill.

Admission to Los Banos cost twenty-five cents, which gave the bather a swimsuit, a towel and a key to the locker room. The indoor concrete "plunge tank" was fifty by one hundred feet. "Pure seawater" filled the tank, heated by steam from the streetcar power plant on E Street, just behind Los Banos. "All the luxuries that a bather could desire, in the way of Turkish baths, plunges, showers, and slides" were provided, reported the *Union*.

Los Banos lasted for many years. But within that time, indoor plumbing was fast making inroads to American homes. Public bathhouses became passé. In 1928, the San Diego Gas and Electric Company tore down Los Banos and expanded the Station B power plant, which survives today at West Broadway and Kettner Boulevard.

# SAN DIEGO STATE'S FIRST YEAR

*We shall not wait until the new building on University Heights is finished before opening the normal school. We have decided to open it in temporary quarters on November 1, with a corps of perhaps five teachers.*
*—Wilfred R. Guy, Chairman, Board of Trustees,*
*San Diego State Normal School*

On November 1, 1898, the first classes of the future San Diego State University began. In leased rooms above a downtown novelty shop, eighty-one students appeared for the formal opening of the new San Diego State Normal School.

San Diegans had clamored for a state-funded teachers training college for years. Called "normal schools" because they instilled teaching norms, the institutions had already been established in San Jose, Los Angeles and Chico. Local boosters lobbied hard in Sacramento to secure a San Diego college—essential, they believed, for the growth of the region's elementary and high schools.

Real estate promoters were also keen on securing a college that would anchor and encourage new development. A College of Arts and Sciences was proposed in 1887 for a new subdivision—optimistically called "University Heights." As a branch of the University of Southern California, classes were held for a short time in a downtown church while construction started at Park Boulevard, but the college soon failed.

In 1894, school promoters got a second chance when sixteen acres of land and buildings in Pacific Beach were offered to the state by a developer

Students wave from the top floor of the Hill Building at Sixth and F Streets in 1898. *Special Collections, San Diego State University.*

in exchange for a school. With the proposed gift as an incentive, San Diego representatives secured state funding for a new normal school for the "training and educating of teachers." The bill was signed by Governor James Budd on March 13, 1897.

As part of the legislation, the school bill authorized a board of trustees that would select the permanent site for the school. Besides the original Pacific Beach offer, there were now competing choices. John D. Spreckels offered a site in his Spreckels Heights development above Old Town, and Escondido proposed the property and buildings of its own high school.

But the trustees were most impressed by University Heights at Park and El Cajon Boulevards. The site of the abortive College of Arts was the unanimous choice of the trustees on June 3, 1897. The firm Hebbard and Gill was selected to design and build the first buildings for a cost not to exceed $100,000. Ground was broken on August 1, 1898.

As Irving Gill's classic Beaux Arts structure began to rise on Park Boulevard, the normal school trustees eagerly announced their intention to open the school as soon as possible in a temporary location yet to be found. Board chairman Wilfred Guy suggested it might be the Marshal-Higgins Block at Fourth and C Streets or possibly rooms at the YMCA at Sixth and D. Chairman Guy would only say, "We want to get the school in good running order as soon as possible and nothing stands in the way of accomplishing that objective."

The trustees published notice in the newspapers inviting potential students to enroll at a downtown law office in the Keating Block for the two-year program. Applicants were expected to "be of good moral character" and have at least a grammar school education. They were required to file a

Samuel T. Black, a former state superintendent of public instruction, served as the first president of the San Diego Normal School. *Special Collections, San Diego State University.*

declaration that they were entering the college "for the purpose of fitting themselves to teach" in public schools. The normal school would offer only three classes at first: English, algebra and history. The trustees apologized that a science class could not be offered owing to the lack of laboratory space and equipment.

First notice of a site came on October 8, only three weeks before the start of classes. The school's new president, Samuel T. Black, the former state superintendent of public instruction, announced that he would establish his office in the Hill Block at Sixth and F Streets, where "the third floor and three rooms on the second floor will be fitted up for a temporary normal school."

The school rooms were "fitted up in fine style," according to the *San Diego Union*. "A notable feature will be the use of tables instead of desks for the students, and is President Black's innovation."

A faculty of five teachers was announced—all well-qualified, experienced instructors. Miss Emma Way accepted the lead job as preceptress, which paid an annual salary of $1,600. As "the moral instructor of the young ladies," Miss Way was expected to dictate "what proper entertainments shall be attended" and also to designate a curfew time for the female students.

On the first day of classes, the students gathered in the assembly room and began their day with the singing of "America." The invocation followed, delivered by Reverend A.E. Knapp. After addresses by President Black and Chairman Guy, the seventy-five young ladies and six young men were assigned rooms, and their studies began. Each day began in similar fashion: a gathering in the assembly room, where the students chanted the Lord's Prayer and sang hymns. The teachers would then take turns reading from the scriptures before the students went to class.

Additional pupils were admitted in February "on account of the crowded conditions of the original classes." With more than one hundred students enrolled, President Black judged the institution in "a very flourishing condition." The lady students greeted the spring with the organization of a rowing club—the school's first sports team.

San Diego State's first year came to a close on June 29, 1899. With 135 students completing classes, the year had "far exceeded the expectations of everyone," President Black declared. "While we have had only eight months' school in which to do a full year's work...work was accomplished in every line, but with one exception." Algebra, the president noted regretfully, had not been finished "because the study requires more time than we could give it."

In the fall of 1899, the San Diego State Normal School began the year at its permanent home on Park Boulevard. The school would graduate its first students that spring: twenty-three women and three men. In 1921, the growing school became the four-year San Diego State Teachers College, and in February 1931, the college moved to its current home on Montezuma Mesa in East San Diego.

PART II

# CIVIC PRIDE

## THE 1890 FEDERAL CENSUS

*"I am incensed," Mayor Douglas Gunn responded on Saturday when the census figure of 15,700 for San Diego was mentioned. "I shall write to the census authorities and the Secretary of Interior demanding a recount."*
—San Diego Union, *July 7, 1890*

The Eleventh U.S. Census officially began on June 2, 1890. In the next few weeks, forty-seven thousand census enumerators spread out across America to pore over town maps, knock on doors and personally visit every house and family in order to tally perhaps the most significant and controversial census the nation had ever seen.

Like most U.S. cities, San Diego looked forward to the decennial counting with optimism, knowing that it would show a major population rise and lead to significantly better legislative representation. Mayor Douglas Gunn estimated that the 1890 count would show a city population of at least 27,000, up from 2,637 in 1880.

A local clothing store, A. Dorsey & Company, displayed its census spirit by announcing prizes "to the best guesser" of the final count. First prize was the choice of any twenty-five-dollar men's suit in the store. Second prize was an eight-dollar Dunlap silk hat, "the very best in the market."

The questionnaire in the hands of San Diego's sixteen enumerators contained twenty-five questions to be asked of every citizen. There was

Fifth Street in the late 1880s showed unpaved streets, but a city was rising with new buildings, horse-drawn trolleys and a modern municipal government. *Special Collections, San Diego Public Library.*

a separate sheet for every family. New entries in 1890 included questions about home ownership and indebtedness, and a query about race asked "whether white, black, mulatto, quadroon, octoroon, Chinese, Japanese, or Indian."

There was little controversy over the questionnaire, but as the numbering got underway in San Diego, city officials quickly became concerned over the pace of the census taking and the completeness of the count. The Census Bureau required that cities of San Diego's size be canvassed within two weeks. The count was particularly sluggish in the red-light district south of H Street, where shy residents tended to ignore the knock on the door.

Mayor Gunn moaned, "This enumeration is of too great importance to have it rushed...I have heard it asserted that the enumerators were going to make out a population something like 6,000 or more short of what it really is. If this is so, irreparable damage will be done to San Diego."

As the enumeration neared its scheduled conclusion in mid-June, San Diegans began coming forward to announce they were uncounted. George B. Hensley, a businessman active in the chamber of commerce, declared that "none of his family had been seen by the census takers and he knew of many families who had been missed." The proprietor of a local hotel complained that "her house was full of guests, none of whom had been counted."

The chamber of commerce voiced its concerns by telegraphing a resolution to the superintendent of the census in Washington, D.C., conveying "earnest protest against the unsystematic, careless and inaccurate manner in which the enumeration of the population of this city is being made."

Some people also refused to be counted. "The enumerators complain that they are rudely treated," reported the *Union*. "One says he was ordered out of three places. As many doors were shut in his face, and eighteen persons positively declined to answer the questions."

On June 19, the *Union* reported that people were being arrested for refusing to answer the census enumerator's questions, per order of Census Supervisor L.E. Mosher from Los Angeles. A deputy U.S. marshal escorted three San Diegans on the train to Los Angeles who seemed "afflicted with much lassitude over the census."

With surprising speed, San Diego's census total arrived on July 7. San Diegans were stunned. According to the U.S. Census, the city's population totaled only 15,700. Mayor Gunn was furious. Charging that two out of three people had been missed, the mayor demanded a recount. He took a train to Los Angeles and complained personally to Supervisor Mosher, who promised to take the matter under advisement.

A few days later, Mosher telegraphed Gunn to say that he would come to San Diego and thoroughly investigate "your claim of errors and omissions in the enumeration." The *Los Angeles Times* headlined the story: "CENSUS SQUABBLING: San Diego Thinks She Is in the Soup."

On July 15, the supervisor arrived and settled in at the Hotel del Coronado. Two days of audits followed in a room at city hall. Mosher's enumerators rechecked their schedules and interviewed more than 200 people who claimed to be uncounted. When the work was over, Mosher's team added 336 names to the tally. San Diego's official population was now 16,037.

With the count official, San Diegans swallowed their pride and looked at the bright side. The percentage increase since 1880 was 512 percent versus "only" 350 percent for Los Angeles. The *Union* noted, "The per cent of increase in population for the last ten years is wonderful to hear, and wonderful to tell." (Unfortunately, the winner of the A. Dorsey & Company "best guesser" contest went unreported.)

San Diegans may have accepted their results, but nationally, the 1890 U.S. Census was controversial. People were shocked (and suspicious) of the speed of the census count. The eleventh census was the first to be counted by machine; the returns were tabulated from data entered on punch cards.

The Hollerith keypunch is shown in this woodcut illustration from *Scientific American*, August 30, 1890.

The rough population estimate for the entire country (62 million) was announced after six weeks of processing. The complete 1880 count had taken eight years.

The 1890 census is mostly remembered as "the lost census." In 1921, about 25 percent of the warehoused census schedules was destroyed in a fire in Washington, D.C. But 75 percent of the forms survived the blaze either damaged or untouched. These irreplaceable returns were stored and ignored before a government order authorized their destruction in 1933.

# THE GREAT RACE

*"Go!" Major General Leonard Wood, chief of staff of the United States army, gave the command...The first automobile in the desperate San Diego–Phoenix race shot forward with a bound.*
*—San Diego Union, October 27, 1912*

In the early 1900s, Southern Californians reveled in auto road racing. One of the most popular events was the annual Los Angeles–Phoenix road race. As a test of fragile machines running on barely existent trails, nothing else compared to the annual dash across the desert.

In October 1912, San Diegans cast envious eyes on Los Angeles as that city prepared for its fifth annual race. Why shouldn't such a race begin in San Diego, the civic boosters asked? After all, Phoenix was a straight shot from San Diego. A successful showing would also highlight San Diego as the logical terminus for the proposed national "Ocean-to-Ocean Highway," stretching from Baltimore, Maryland, to California.

A committee led by San Diego businessman and road enthusiast Ed Fletcher proposed to challenge Los Angeles with its own race, starting on the same date and time. Prize money was quickly raised—much of it from the city of Phoenix, which was delighted with the San Diego bid.

Official sanction for the event came from the American Automobile Association (AAA). The races would begin at about the same time, but the Los Angeles drivers would reach Arizona by way of San Bernardino and Indio before turning southwest to Yuma. The San Diego racers would go due east. Despite a detour north after El Centro to avoid several miles of sand hills, the southern path was at least one hundred miles shorter than the Los Angeles route. "We will beat the Los Angeles cars by a full twelve hours, at the very least," boasted one San Diego driver.

For the most part, Los Angeles ignored the race preparations in San Diego. The *Times* barely acknowledged its southern neighbor. The *Los Angeles Examiner* was more enthusiastic and challenged Ed Fletcher to a separate "pathfinder" race between the two cities. Starting earlier in the day than the official entrants, the *Examiner* car would race to Phoenix via Blythe, ignoring Yuma. Fletcher, represented by the *San Diego Evening Tribune*, would follow the more direct route due east across the desert. When the *Phoenix Gazette* joined in as a cosponsor of Fletcher, the car became the "Tribune-Gazette Pathfinder."

The great race began on Saturday night, October 26. Enormous crowds filled the sidewalks and streets as twenty-two growling race cars lined up on Fifth Street

"Pathfinder" Ed Fletcher drove a twenty-horsepower, air-cooled Franklin to lead the San Diego racers. *Special Collections, University of California–San Diego.*

Fording the Agua Fria River on the way to Phoenix challenged the road racers. *Special Collections, University of California–San Diego.*

between D and C Streets. At 10:15 p.m., the celebrity starter—Major General Leonard Wood, hero of the Spanish-American War—yelled "Go," and the first car "shot forward with a bound." At five-minute intervals, the rest of the field started on their way, speeding up Fifth to University and then east out of town on El Cajon Boulevard.

Up north, only twelve cars began the traditional Los Angeles–Phoenix version of the great race. According to the *Times*, "tens of thousands of frenzied men and women" gathered for the start in front of the Hollenbeck Hotel. At 11:00 p.m., the drivers began "the most sensational fight ever waged on the sand of the lonely desert" as they sped east toward Ontario and then southeast into the desert.

The last two cars to start that night were the "outlaws." Running their own separate match race—unsanctioned by the AAA—were San Diego mayor James Wadham and future mayor Percy J. Benbough. At 12:05 a.m. on Sunday morning, the big touring cars, each carrying three passengers besides the driver, set off toward Arizona for the "honor and glory" of San Diego.

One car was already well on the way to Phoenix. "Pathfinder" Ed Fletcher, driving a twenty-horsepower, air-cooled Franklin, had left early Saturday morning. Fletcher and his three companions decided to ignore the detour taken by the San Diego racers (north toward Niland, to avoid the towering sand dunes east of El Centro) and risk the more direct path, straight through the sand to Yuma. But first Fletcher had to drive through thirty miles of scrubby desert. "The Franklin did nobly," Fletcher recalled, but he found that eventually small twigs filled his engine and began popping through his cooling system. Fletcher stopped the car and lifted the hood, and the twigs blazed. The men frantically threw sand on the engine to stop the fire.

To negotiate the sand hills, Fletcher reduced his tire pressure to twenty pounds. He had also prudently stationed a horse team in the area. When the car labored in the hub-deep sand, the six-horse team pulled his touring car four and a half miles across the dunes.

It was dark by the time the pathfinder car reached the Colorado River, opposite Yuma. With the ferryboat gone for the night, Fletcher tried the railroad bridge. "We took that risk; used blankets and seats to keep [the rail spikes] from puncturing our tires—but we made it."

Fletcher's next obstacle was the weather. Heavy winds and rain beat down as they reached the Hassayampa River, flowing at flood stage but negotiable on another railroad bridge. Downed eucalyptus trees on the trail also slowed their progress. The men sawed through the trees and continued on. Outside Phoenix, the Agua Fria River was crossed by yet another convenient railroad bridge.

Fletcher finally drove into Phoenix—"exhausted but happy"—nineteen and a half hours after leaving San Diego. The competing *Examiner* pathfinder car never arrived. It had broken down in the desert near Blythe. The next cars to appear in Phoenix were the "outlaws." Mayor Wadham pulled in at 5:40 a.m. on Monday morning. Percy Benbough arrived two hours later, bemoaning a delay stuck in the sand but claiming a better running time than Wadham. The two men bickered over the result and then agreed to call it a tie.

The official drivers from San Diego and Los Angeles—all delayed by a checkpoint in Yuma—began coming in that afternoon. Only seven San Diegans finished the hard race. D.C. Campbell, driving a Stevens-Duryea, was first with a running time of sixteen hours, fifty-nine minutes.

Los Angeles's best finish was by Ralph Hamlin in eighteen hours, forty-five minutes. The *Times* reported his victory with a stirring story of Hamlin's race. The *San Diego Union* proudly headlined its account, "SAN DIEGO CAR BEATS LOS ANGELES."

# WONDERLAND

*With one swift move of the hand at the big switchboard at "Wonderland" last night, Mayor Charles F. O'Neall of San Diego opened the big playground at Ocean Beach just as the clock struck seven. The blaze of light that followed was a startler to the crowds that were waiting outside the closed gates clamoring for admittance.*

–San Diego Union, *July 3, 1913*

The public sneak preview of Wonderland, two days before its scheduled July 4 opening, delighted thousands of visitors. When Mayor O'Neall threw the switch, twenty-two thousand tungsten lights illuminated the new amusement park at Ocean Beach. The entrance gates—framed by towering minarets—opened, and the throngs poured in, accompanied by a band playing "America."

For the official opening on July 4, the park added fireworks, with music from the Royal Marine Band. "The Battle in the Clouds" ran all day and into

The entrance to Wonderland of Ocean Beach. *Special Collections, San Diego Public Library.*

the evening, directed by Signor Paglia, the "famous master of pyrotechnics" and former director of displays for the king of Italy.

More than twenty thousand people came on opening day. The Point Loma Railroad Company ran streetcars every twenty minutes from Fourth and Broadway for the forty-minute trip to Ocean Beach. Buses from Horton Plaza ferried people to the park, one vehicle every thirty minutes.

San Diegans had never seen anything like it. "The most carefully planned and constructed amusement park on the Pacific coast" was built at the cost of $300,000 on eight acres of concrete-paved land south of Voltaire, between Abbott Street and the ocean. Wonderland boasted "40 attractions," including a dance pavilion, a bowling alley, a half-acre children's playground, a roller skating rink and a seawater bathing plunge. A zoo featured lions, bears, leopards, wolves, mountain lions, a hyena and fifty-six varieties of monkeys—all housed and "waiting for the givers of peanuts and popcorn."

The fun zone—on the model of Coney Island's famed Luna Park—included a water slide, a carousel, carnival games and the biggest roller coaster on the Pacific Coast. The wooden coaster, called the Blue Streak Racer, ran two cars, which raced each other on parallel tracks over a 3,500-foot-long course.

Chute-the-Chutes was a popular steep waterslide ride. *Special Collections, San Diego Public Library.*

Reflecting the conservative mores of the day, the family-oriented Wonderland was advertised as "morally clean," safe and wholesome. Violators of respectability risked expulsion. "There will be no 'mashing' anywhere in the park," the management declared. Unseemly behavior in the Waldorf Ballroom required particular vigilance. To ensure that there was no "turkey-trotting" or "bunny-hugging" on the dance floor, a Mrs. Margaret Madden kept a watchful eye.

Ruth Varney Held, in her 1975 book *Beach Town*, recalled her experience at Wonderland as a seven-year-old:

> *I was there, starry-eyed. I paid my ten cents at the booth between the fancy towers, drifted in, and gasped in awe...Monkeyland charmed me first, with 350 monkeys making funny faces and reaching for tidbits. One was the mischievous Mr. Spider, advertised as "The oldest monkey in captivity," who might reach out through the bars with his tail and whisk your hat off. My next love was the Chute-the-Chutes, a high, steep water-slide. Flat-bottomed boats shoved off from the top, to whoosh down into the pool below, spraying water over the shrieking passengers.*

Held marveled at the apparent success of the park, noting that "one of the great wonders of Wonderland was how San Diego could support such a large amusement park." After all, the population of San Diego barely exceeded sixty-five thousand, and Ocean Beach had perhaps three hundred people.

Against such odds, Wonderland thrived for only two seasons. For all their careful planning, the operators of the park failed to consider the prospect of competition. The opening of the Panama-California Exposition in 1915 slashed attendance, and the park fell into foreclosure. In March 1915, Wonderland was sold at auction.

To add insult to injury, turbulent ocean tides undermined the foundations of the giant rollercoaster and closed the park's premier attraction in January 1916. The Blue Streak Racer was dismantled and shipped to Santa Monica, where it ran at the Pleasure Pier for many years.

The most enduring legacy of Wonderland would be its small zoo. When the Panama-California fair began in Balboa Park, the menagerie was rented to the exposition company for $40 per day. Housed in a series of cages near Indian Village on Park Boulevard, the collection of animals was eventually sold to the city for $500. The well-traveled animals would appear again when the San Diego Zoo opened in 1922.

# BABE RUTH IN SAN DIEGO

*George Herman Ruth, world's greatest baseball player, came into our midst on the noon train today slanting one eye at his traveling bag and the other at the overcast sky. "Low visibility," quoth the Babe. "But if the raindrops will stay away for a short time I guess I can get the range and park a few baseballs on the far side of your famous stadium."*

–San Diego Tribune, *October 29, 1924*

The most celebrated player in baseball history was a frequent visitor to San Diego. "Babe" Ruth made several trips to the city as an exhibition ballplayer, performed in a local theater show and, for time, even contemplated building a home in La Mesa.

Ruth first visited San Diego on December 28, 1919, only two days after his famous sale to the New York Yankees by the Boston Red Sox. Already a prolific home run hitter at age twenty-four, Ruth had finished the 1919 season with a record twenty-nine home runs, a mark he would improve repeatedly in the following fifteen years as a Yankee.

Home run hitter Babe Ruth delighted San Diegans with his off-season appearances at City Stadium. *Library of Congress*.

Ruth's visit was the first of many "barnstorming" tours he would make across the country following the end of the regular major-league season. The games were hugely popular in every town, where Ruth and fellow big leaguers would play with local amateurs. Batting exhibitions preceded each contest, ensuring Ruthian home runs, even when the Babe failed to hit one out during a game. Many games never finished because fans tended to swamp the field in the late innings to meet their hero up close.

In the Sunday afternoon game at the City Stadium (later known as Balboa Stadium), Ruth's "All-Stars" beat a San Diego amateur team, 15–7. Ruth (an outfielder for the Yankees) played first base, where he "bungled a couple" of chances, according to a *Tribune* reporter. But he redeemed himself in the ninth inning when he delivered what the crowd of 6,500 had come see: a home run that "soared and sailed like a shot" an estimated four hundred feet.

Ruth returned to San Diego five years later, near the finish of a fifteen-city tour. The weather had been rainy on October 29, 1924, but a "liberal supply of sawdust in the wet spots" made the field playable. Nearly three thousand fans braved the chilly breeze at City Stadium, paying seventy-five cents for adults and twenty-five cents for children under twelve.

In the pregame warm-ups, Ruth and his Yankee teammate Bob Meusel put on a home run clinic, driving several balls into the concrete stands. Reporters noted that "Ruth has a very peculiar stance at the plate, and certainly takes a terrific 'cut' at the ball." In the game itself, Ruth had four hits and no homers, but his team beat the "San Diegos," 10–6.

Between innings, "hundreds of youngsters" swarmed the bench to get Ruth's autograph on "a baseball, card, or piece of paper." A reporter noted that Ruth played the entire game with a pencil behind his ear, "ready for instant use."

The Babe made a winter visit to San Diego in 1927 to work a one-week vaudeville engagement at the Pantages Theatre on Fifth and B Streets. The week of January 10, Ruth performed three shows per day, giving hitting demonstrations and performing a skit that celebrated his recent baseball feats. Each show concluded with the Babe's invitation to kids to come on stage and receive autographed baseballs.

Apart from his three-a-days at the Pantages, Ruth kept a hectic leisure schedule in the company of friends: playing golf at the Coronado Country Club, duck hunting on Sweetwater Lake and deep-sea fishing off Point Loma. Ruth also found time to purchase a La Mesa homesite in the new Windsor Hills tract on the southern slope of Mount Nebo. Ruth decided to hold the lot for investment purposes, being "sold" on San Diego.

Yankee slugger Babe Ruth with a young fan at City Stadium, October 29, 1924. *San Diego History Center.*

The January visit had a strange epilogue. When Ruth traveled to Long Beach for another vaudeville show, he was met by sheriff's deputies and arrested. A warrant was served for violating child labor laws in San Diego. A zealous deputy state labor commissioner, Stanley Gue, had accused Ruth of making children a part of his act at the Pantages without obtaining required work permits. A second violation charged him with keeping the children on stage after a 10:00 p.m. curfew. Ruth posted $500 bail and departed for New York. The next month, a San Diego judge dismissed the charges and ridiculed Commissioner Gue for demanding licenses for children "to step up onto a stage to get a free baseball."

Under happier circumstances, Ruth returned to San Diego in October. The slugger had just finished a triumphant Yankees season with a World Series title and a new record of sixty homers—a mark that would stand for thirty-four years. The Babe's visit came near the end of a nine-state, twenty-one-city tour. On this trip, he was joined by a rising young Yankees star, Lou Gehrig. Babe wore a tour uniform of all black, with white lettering emblazoned "Bustin' Babes." Gehrig's white uniform was lettered in black with "Larrupin' Lous."

In the October 28 game, sponsored by the American Legion, Ruth's team beat Gehrig's, 3–2. Competition for souvenir baseballs hit by the "Homerun Twins" was fierce. "Every time that Ruth or Gehrig cracked one off the diamond, it was a signal for hundreds of the youngsters to make for the spot on the run, and then would follow a free-for-all struggle for possession of the prized agate."

Ruth's last appearance in San Diego was witnessed by 3,500 fans. The afternoon game was called on account of darkness at the end of the seventh inning. The fans were satisfied. "There were no home runs hit," the *Union* reported with regret, "but the two Yankee sluggers gave a mighty account of themselves just the same."

# THE "STOLEN" CABRILLO STATUE

*"I didn't steal it," declared Senator Fletcher with ruffled dignity. "But there were threats of lawsuit and an injunction, so with a gang of men, a derrick and a truck, I took quick action, and possession is nine points of the law."*
—Los Angeles Times, *March 1, 1940*

For more than six decades, the figure of Juan Rodríguez Cabrillo has watched over San Diego Bay from the heights of Cabrillo National Monument on Point Loma. The fourteen-foot sculpture is an icon to San Diegans, who know Cabrillo as the sailor who entered our port in 1542, the first European to visit California.

A statue commemorating Cabrillo had long been sought by San Diegans, particularly by the Portuguese community, which claimed the explorer as one of its own. In the 1930s, the artist Alvaro de Bree was commissioned by Portugal to create the now familiar sandstone sculpture. A decade of controversy would follow.

As a gift to the State of California, the Cabrillo statue was sent to San Francisco in 1939 for the Golden Gate International Exposition. But it arrived too late for display and languished instead in a federal customs warehouse. A six-foot replica served as a stand-in at the fair.

The statue of explorer Juan Rodríguez Cabrillo at Cabrillo National Monument on Point Loma. *Carol M. Highsmith Archive, Library of Congress.*

After the exposition's conclusion, Governor Culbert Olson formally accepted Portugal's gift. Released from the customhouse, the statue was sent for safekeeping to a private residence in the bay area. The ultimate destination, decided Governor Olson, would be the city of Oakland in Alameda County, home to more than sixty thousand people of Portuguese descent.

The governor's decision outraged San Diegans, who believed that the most appropriate site for the statue would be the port where Juan Cabrillo originally landed. The community was also anxious to make the figure the centerpiece of a planned Cabrillo celebration, marking the 400th anniversary of the explorer's visit to California. Joseph Dryer, president of the Heaven on Earth Club, enlisted the aid of California senator Ed Fletcher to bring the Cabrillo statue to San Diego.

The statue "was a prize worth fighting for," thought Fletcher. The senator took the offensive, securing a legal opinion from his Sacramento colleagues that held that the legislature—not the governor—would determine the permanent home of the statue.

Next, with the aid of Lawrence Oliver, founder of San Diego's Portuguese-American Club, Fletcher located the statue at the home of a former Portuguese national near San Francisco. Fletcher and his wife, accompanied by Senator George Biggar and his wife, paid a visit to the house, where the crated, seven-ton statue lay on the floor of the garage. "It was so heavy it had broken the concrete in the garage floor. We discussed the matter with the lady, found she was sympathetic, and convinced her the statue should go to San Diego. Her husband having died recently, she wanted it out of the garage, but insisted upon some authority from the state before having it moved to San Diego permanently."

Fletcher introduced a bill in the state Senate that designated San Diego as the permanent home of the Cabrillo statue. The senators passed the resolution unanimously, but it died in an assembly committee, killed by an assemblyman from Oakland. Fletcher's only thought was to get possession of the statue.

Armed with a letter of authorization from the State Park Commission and a copy of the *State Journal* showing the approval of the Senate, Fletcher returned to the house. The widow viewed the "documentary proof" and consented to the statue's removal.

Earlier in the day, Fletcher had arranged for movers to be ready at a moment's notice. Now he called in the movers, and a crew of four arrived with a "tremendous" truck. The men hefted the statue onto rollers and pushed it out to the sidewalk. Then the telephone rang:

> *She called me into the house and asked me to talk over the phone to the Vice-Consul of Portugal who protested its removal and threatened court proceedings. I also got another telephone call from an attorney in Oakland who threatened an injunction. The lady was in tears, but it was too late. I promised her she would never regret it and left with the statue.*

Fletcher's crew hauled the statue to the Santa Fe railroad depot and put it on an evening train for San Diego. The statue was soon safely locked up in a San Diego warehouse under the care of City Manager Fred Rhodes.

The uproar was immediate. Oakland's Portuguese community demanded an investigation. Alameda assemblyman George P. Miller filed a protest with Governor Olson, and the governor himself publicly accused Senator Fletcher of "kidnapping" Cabrillo. The furor slowly died as bills introduced in the legislature to retrieve the statue were defeated in committee.

San Diego dedicated the statue on the grounds of the Naval Training Center near Harbor Drive in December 1940. Here the sculpture remained for the next several years, behind a fence and out of public view. Plans for the statue's starring role in the Cabrillo quadricentennial ended when the festival was canceled due to World War II. Instead, a simple ceremony honoring Cabrillo was held on September 28, 1942. Dr. Reginald Poland, director of the San Diego Fine Arts Gallery, praised the statue as "a fine work of art" and "a fortunate balance of the natural and abstract."

The statue was finally moved to Cabrillo National Monument in 1949, where it was erected on a five-foot pedestal north of the lighthouse. An elaborate rededication ceremony on September 28 honored the "discoverer" of San Diego. The statue would later be moved closer to the visitor center at a spot overlooking the harbor.

Time would not be kind to the sandstone sculpture. Weathering badly in the ocean air and suffering from "visitor abuse," it was brought indoors for restoration in the 1980s, never to return. An exact replica sculpted out of denser limestone was dedicated in 1988.

Today, the figure of Cabrillo still stirs controversy. The assumed Portuguese nativity of Juan Cabrillo is doubted; many historians now believe that the navigator was Spanish. Scholars also question the statue's appearance, finding

the presentation unauthentic. Without question, though, the storied statue continues to be a star attraction for one of the most visited national monuments in the country.

San Diego dedicated the Cabrillo statue on the grounds of the Naval Training Center in December 1940, where it remained hidden from public view for the next several years. *Special Collections, San Diego Public Library.*

# PART III

# SAN DIEGO AT WAR

## SAN DIEGO'S WARSHIP

*On Wednesday morning the United State cruiser San Diego will be formally rechristened in San Diego's harbor….No city on the California coast has been so signally honored by the government, and the fact that a modern war vessel with its hundreds of men will carry the name of San Diego to all parts of the United States and the world is worthy of a celebration.*
                    –San Diego Union, *September 14, 1914*

With a gala ceremony in San Diego Harbor, the flagship cruiser of the Pacific fleet was christened with style. Thousands watched as the daughter of the mayor, six-year-old Miss Annie May O'Neall, undraped a canvas over the stern, revealing the name "San Diego." Mayor O'Neall proudly declared the day a city holiday. A barbecue honoring the ship's sailors was held in Balboa Park, and the officers and their ladies were treated to a grand ball at the U.S. Grant Hotel.

The USS *San Diego* was the new name for a heavy armored cruiser that had been launched ten years earlier as the *California*. Built in San Francisco by the famed Union Iron Works, the ship was 505 feet in length and 70 feet in width and displaced 13,600 tons. Coal-fired steam engines turned two eighteen-foot diameter propellers and powered the ship to a top speed of twenty-two knots.

The battleship USS *San Diego*, circa 1916. *National Photo Company Collection, Library of Congress.*

The cruiser was a *Pennsylvania*-class ship, one of the most potent warships in the world. Its armament included four eight-inch guns, fourteen six-inch guns and an assortment of rapid-fire weapons and torpedo tubes. Nearly nine hundred men and officers served aboard ship. The gun crew was the proud holder of the Spokane Trophy, an annual award given the ship with the best marksmanship in the navy.

The ship's name change came as the navy began building a new series of super-dreadnoughts that would all be named after states. San Diego congressman William Kettner alertly contacted friends in the Department of the Navy and pushed for the "San Diego" name on the *California*, which would soon lose its name to a new battleship. The secretary of the navy approved the request, and San Diego had its first namesake warship.

Serving in the eastern Pacific, often as the fleet's flagship, the *San Diego* would anchor frequently in the city. The ship was a popular attraction in 1915–16 as the city held its world's fair, the Panama-California Exposition.

On January 21, 1915, the ship suffered near disaster while cruising in the Gulf of California near La Paz, Mexico. Ensign Robert Cary was taking readings of the steam and air pressure in the boilers. He had just finished inspection of fire room no. 2 when the boilers exploded. Cary quickly returned to the room and grabbed the watertight doors, which were being closed electronically from the bridge. With scalding steam erupting around him, he held the doors open long enough for the men inside the room to escape.

One of the men escaping from the burning room was a young Filipino seaman, Telesforo Trinidad. When Trinidad realized that one seaman had been left behind in the room, he returned and picked up the injured seaman. As boilers in another fire room exploded, Trinidad handed off the injured man and assisted in the rescue of more men from the fire room.

For their extraordinary heroism, Ensign Cary and Fireman Trinidad would be awarded the Medal of Honor, the nation's highest decoration for valor. Trinidad was the first sailor of Asian descent to win the award. Cary would continue as an officer in the navy and retire in 1945 as a rear admiral.

Nine seamen were reported killed in the accident. The wounded ship steamed to Guaymas for temporary repairs and then proceeded to San Francisco to spend several weeks at the Mare Island Navy Yard. The *San Diego* returned to active duty in the fall, and on November 6, 1915, the crew rescued forty-eight passengers from the schooner *Fort Bragg*, wrecked on a reef twenty miles northeast of Cape San Lucas.

After the entry of the United States in World War I, the *San Diego* was ordered in July 1917 to join the Atlantic Fleet. After passing through the Panama Canal, the ship joined the fleet at Hampton Roads. For the next year, the cruiser escorted convoys across the submarine-infested North Atlantic—never losing a ship under its watch.

On the morning of July 19, 1918, the *San Diego* was headed for New York from the Portsmouth Navy Yard in New Hampshire. Zigzagging south in calm seas, the cruiser was a few miles off Long Island when a crewman spotted a periscope above the waves. Minutes later, the crew felt a dull thud on the port side. Two explosions followed, and with the port side ripped open, the ship began to list.

Captain Harley Christy pointed the *San Diego* toward shore and tried to beach the ship on Fire Island. It never made it. With the cruiser sinking fast, Captain Christy gave the order to abandon ship. Most of the nearly 1,200 men and officers got off in lifeboats; others dived off the hull with only their life jackets. Twenty-eight minutes after the initial blast, the ship rolled over and sank.

News of the sinking reached San Diego quickly. The *Union* announced the next day: "Destruction of the armored cruiser San Diego by a Hun submarine created universal sorrow throughout the city...According to the best information available last night there were 25 San Diego boys serving on the cruiser when she was torpedoed."

Despite the newspaper's assumption, the cause of the sinking was a mystery at first. The sailors were convinced that a torpedo had hit them. In fact, German U-boats had recently been in the area planting surface mines. *U-156*, it was ultimately decided, had laid a floating mine that was struck by the *San Diego*. The secondary explosions were boilers bursting. Three men were killed on the ship, and three more died in the water.

A local drive to get the name "San Diego" attached to a new cruiser began and then foundered. In 1942, longtime efforts finally succeeded with the commissioning of the antiaircraft light cruiser *San Diego*. The new ship earned fifteen battle stars in World War II, fighting in major battles such Guadalcanal, Tarawa, Iwo Jima and Okinawa. It was removed from the navy list in 1959 and scrapped.

The first USS *San Diego* lies today in 110 feet of water, 13.5 miles south of Fire Island Inlet. Listed on the National Register of Historic Places, it is one of the best-known shipwrecks on the East Coast and attracts hundreds of scuba divers each year.

# THE GERMAN RAIDER

A front-page headline in the *San Diego Union* screamed the news: "AMERICAN GUNBOAT TAKES HUN RAIDER OFF MEXICAN COAST." Less than a year after America's entry into World War I, San Diegans were riveted by reports of a captured German raider ship set "to create havoc with Pacific coast shipping."

Three U.S. Navy gunboats had taken their prize fifteen miles off the coast of Mazatlan on March 19, 1918. "Heavily armed" and reportedly flying the flag of the kaiser's Imperial Navy, the "German corsair" had surrendered after a navy cruiser fired a shot across its bow. Its German crew had tried to cripple the ship by destroying the engines, but an American warship had the boat under tow, now destined for San Diego.

Americans in 1918 were willing to believe the worst about their wartime enemy, including stories of vast German conspiracies from Mexico. "It is a well known fact," the *Union* decided, "that thousands of Germans throughout Mexico, who have been constantly intriguing against the United States, cheerfully would expend hundreds of thousands of dollars to assist in the work of outfitting German corsairs for the purpose of preying on Pacific coast commerce."

The schooner *Alexander Agassiz* after its capture on March 19, 1918. *Naval Historical Foundation.*

As a "German corsair," the captured ship seemed an unlikely choice. The alleged raider was an eighty-five-foot schooner named the *Alexander Agassiz*. Many San Diegans remembered the ship. Built locally in 1907 as a research vessel, scientists from the Scripps Institution had used the *Agassiz* for a decade before selling it to three Los Angeles investors for use as a coastal trading ship in Mexico.

Two of the new owners sailed south from San Diego in January 1917 and began their trading business on Mexico's west coast. They were poor businessmen, apparently, and fell quickly into debt. They decided to sell the schooner, but the third owner—a woman named Maude Lochrane—decided to rescue her investment and headed for Mazatlan.

In her mid-thirties, Lochrane was described by the *Los Angeles Times* as "a virile young woman with flaming red hair…an adventurous spirit with an abundance of experience and plenty of nerve." But the bold "mystery woman of the *Agassiz*" was unable to straighten out the finances and soon became desperate.

A German navy officer named Fritz Bauman appeared on the scene. Formerly interned at Angel Island in San Francisco as an enemy alien, Bauman had moved to Mexico after being released. In Mazatlan, Bauman met the distressed Miss Lochrane and somehow managed to gain control of the *Agassiz*.

With a crew of German sailors, Bauman overhauled the little schooner—recaulking the hull, rebuilding the auxiliary engines, adding new sails and preparing the vessel for a career as a raider. The plan, according to witnesses in a later federal court trial, was for the *Agassiz* to pick up guns and ammunition cached on nearby Venados Island and then "capture a Pacific mail boat running to Panama, outfit it with heavier guns than could be mounted on the *Agassiz*, recruit a full crew from pro-Germans now living at West Coast Mexican ports, and then start out on a reign of terror."

Bauman was well aware of U.S. Navy ships patrolling the waters off Mexico. But he believed that the *Alexander Agassiz* would be ignored by the warships as an inoffensive, "hapless trader." He was wrong. As the *Agassiz* dashed from the harbor on the morning of March 19, the U.S. Navy was waiting. Scuttlebutt from the Mazatlan waterfront had alerted the navy to the possible raider. The cruiser *Brutus*, the patrol boat *Vicksburg* and the submarine chaser *SC-302* quickly corralled the fleeing schooner. A signal from the *Brutus* told the *Agassiz* to heave to. When the schooner's crew refused, the cruiser fired a three-inch shell across the bow, and the raider stopped its engines.

As navy ships closed on the *Agassiz*, the small crew "labored like Trojans throwing overboard everything that they thought would be incriminating." When the sailors boarded the schooner, they found one German seaman hiding in the ship's bottom, holding a revolver. He was quickly disarmed. A small quantity of guns was recovered, as well as several German flags. Captured as prisoners of war were five Germans, six Mexicans, the anxious Mexican wife of the *Agassiz* engineer and one befuddled woman from Los Angeles: Miss Maude Lochrane.

"The Germans aboard the cruiser are a hard looking lot," the *Union* reported as the *Agassiz* and *Brutus* anchored in San Diego on March 27. "They are manacled and under the constant guard of a bluejacket guard who pace back and forth near the men with fixed bayonets. The two women are being allowed the freedom of the gun deck."

After hearings in a prize court held in the federal building in early April, the five German prisoners were taken to Los Angeles and locked in the county jail. The Mexican nationals were released, and Maude Lochrane

A "hard looking lot" of German prisoners aboard the USS *Vicksburg*. *Naval Historical Foundation.*

was freed without bail. Miss Lochrane, unfortunately, was soon rearrested after she reportedly "indulged in so many uncomplimentary remarks about President Wilson that it was thought best to put her in jail until the trial of the crew."

Three *Agassiz* crewmen, all charged with espionage, were taken to Fort MacArthur in San Pedro to be interned for the remainder of the war. All others were exonerated, including Maude Lochrane, who briefly regained ownership of the schooner and then lost it again in bankruptcy. The *Alexander Agassiz* found work as a bit player in a "blood and thunder" sea drama for the Famous Players–Lasky film studio before ending its days running aground in San Francisco Bay in 1920.

# The Navy Swimming Pool
# in Balboa Park

*We would rather sacrifice every fish and lily pond in the city than to know
that some young man had lost his life in the service of our country, because
of insufficient training…as a swimmer.*
*—Merchants Association of San Diego, February 5, 1918*

With America's late entry into the fighting of World War I, patriotic San
Diegans rushed to offer proper training facilities for the U.S. military. In
Balboa Park, vacant exposition buildings were transferred to the navy, which
quickly remodeled the structures east of the Plaza de Panama for military
use. By early 1918, more than four thousand navy recruits were stationed in
the park's newly created Naval Training Center.

Stretching over five hundred acres of parkland, the camp had ample room in
a beautiful environment. But the three-mile distance from the waterfront limited
the opportunity for "nautical instruction afloat." Costlier still was the navy's
discovery that 40 percent of the "embryonic sailors" could not swim. In a city
that lacked a single municipal swimming pool, the service had a problem.

A makeshift solution soon appeared. Eyeing the murky, dirt-bottom
lily pond in front of the wood lath Botanical Building, the navy suggested
using the 195- by 43-foot basin for swimming and boating lessons. Balboa
Park's governing Board of Park Commissioners—eager to please its military
guests—"hastened to comply." Unfortunately, the commissioners got cold
feet when news of the request "got abroad."

As a navy report explained, "An element of esthetic nature-lovers made
loud protest against the destruction of the water-lilies with which the pool
was liberally bestrewn." Pressured from "city beautiful" advocates, the
commissioners regretfully announced that they could "not approve the
destruction of one of the Park's most attractive settings" without informing
the taxpayers of the city of the numerous problems the proposal presented.

The lily pond was too shallow for swimming lessons, the commissioners
decided, and the water was too cold. The cost of the fresh water was also a
problem—"an enormous drain upon the city's water supply," they reported.
Instead, the commissioners suggested waiting for a saltwater bathhouse,
currently being constructed on San Diego Bay at the foot of Date Street by
the city's Playgrounds Department.

The camp commandant, Commodore S.W. Wallace, decided to make a
quick public relations campaign to "put the matter in its right light." Speaking

Swimming lessons for navy seaman in Balboa Park's lily pond. *Special Collections, San Diego Public Library.*

to women's clubs, business associations and the press, the commodore called attention "to the relative values of the lives of water-lilies and the lives of American sailors."

The plea from Commodore Wallace was quickly endorsed by San Diego civic clubs and the newspapers. "Give the Boys a Chance," the *Union* editorialized. "Swimming is a very essential part of naval training. A sailor who cannot swim is a sailor whose life is constantly in extra danger."

On February 8, 1918, the chastised park commissioners unanimously voted to turn the lily pond over to the naval camp for use as a swimming pool. A navy officer announced that instruction for the sailors would begin as soon as the plants were removed from the pool and the goldfish placed in another pond. The four-and-a-half-foot-deep pool was "just right for the first steps in swimming."

Transforming a lagoon into a swimming pool turned out to be more complicated than first thought. After draining the pond, the navy decided to slightly deepen the basin and add a concrete lining. Pipes were connected so the water—450,000 gallons of it—could be changed each day.

By May, the swimming lessons were finally underway for up to forty men at one time. First-Class boatswain's mate Alfonso Racicot taught the men the breast stroke and the "double over hand stroke." The sailors took instruction for thirty minutes each day until they could swim unassisted for five minutes. Additional strokes were taught as the men progressed.

With less success, the navy also attempted lessons in boat handling. In the pool barely large enough for swimming, the boat had to be moored in place by the bow and stern while the sailors pulled the oars on the stationary vessel.

After the war's end in November, the navy training camp closed. The sailors' swimming pool became a lily pond once again. Remarkably, the pool experiment was repeated in World War II, as convalescent patients from the U.S. Naval Hospital enjoyed their "swimmin' hole" in the pond temporarily emptied of lily pads and goldfish.

# SPRECKELS'S YACHT

*Skipper Spreckels was happy: he now had a yacht large enough to go wherever he had a fancy to go, comfortable and luxurious enough to enable him to entertain his chosen friends in his own big-hearted way.*
—*H. Austin Adams,* The Man John D. Spreckels *(1924)*

In the early 1900s, the ultimate status symbol for a business tycoon in America was a luxurious, oceangoing yacht. A personal mark of opulence in San Diego was the 226-foot steam yacht *Venetia*, owned by John Diedrich Spreckels.

The city's leading businessman—owner of the local water supply, the streetcar system, the Hotel del Coronado, the *San Diego Union* and many other properties—acquired the yacht in 1910 from Philadelphia financier William W. Elkins. The seven-year-old, Scotland-built *Venetia* had gone through four owners before Spreckels's purchase. He would enjoy the yacht for the next sixteen years, minus a dramatic nineteen-month period during which the *Venetia* went to war for the U.S. Navy.

Spreckels decided to bring his new purchase to California himself. Leaving New York Harbor on October 3, 1910, Spreckels and his family and guests began a leisurely six-month passage to San Diego, with detours to New Orleans and the West Indies before reaching the Pacific via the Straits of Magellan.

It was a comfortable voyage. The steel-hulled yacht with hardwood-lined quarters featured ten staterooms with adjoining bathrooms (and taps for both fresh and salt water). The main deckhouse contained a smoking room and a library in the forward compartment; an elegant dining saloon came next,

John D. Spreckels. *From H. Austin Adams's* The Man John D. Spreckels *(Frye & Smith, 1924).*

followed by the pantry and galley. In the social lounge in the after end, the passengers listened to music from a Weber pianola, sometimes played by Spreckels himself. The rooms were connected by an interior passageway, central steam heat kept the passengers warm in colder latitudes and a crew of thirty attended to every passenger whim.

The *Venetia* docked in San Diego on March 5, 1911. After a few days, the yacht continued on to San Francisco, where Spreckels made a few modifications to his prize. The coal-burning engines were converted to run on oil. California oil was cheaper than East Coast coal, and with new 1,200-barrel oil tanks, the *Venetia*'s cruising range was increased.

In the next several years, Spreckels used the *Venetia* for frequent business trips to San Francisco—as often as every two or three weeks, according to his biographer, H. Austin Adams. After moving to San Diego following San Francisco's great earthquake and fire of 1906, Spreckels usually commuted by train between San Diego and his offices in San Francisco. But Spreckels loathed travel by land. The *Venetia* allowed travel by water, which he loved. The two-day runs at sea "washed his mind clean" and "refreshed his heart," according to Adams.

Spreckels gave up his much-loved yacht upon America's entry into World War I. Leased to the navy as a patrol craft, the *Venetia* was commissioned at Mare Island, San Francisco, on October 15, 1917. The navy remade Spreckels's pleasure boat into an armed gunboat. Torpedoes were added along with four three-inch guns and two antiaircraft machine guns. With a crew of sixty-nine officers and men, the *Venetia* reached the Mediterranean

Sea in March 1918. For the remaining months of the war, the armed yacht protected merchant convoys against U-boat attacks.

The first combat action came on May 11. Covering a convoy bound for Gibraltar, an enemy torpedo streaked past the *Venetia's* bow and struck a French steamship, the SS *Susette Fraisinette*. While the merchantman slowly sank, the *Venetia* drove off *UB-52*, dropping thirteen depth charges on the submerged U-boat. Only days later, the *Venetia* and another gunboat fought off another U-boat that sank a British freighter.

Another major battle came in July. With four other escort ships, the *Venetia* helped screen a convoy of seventeen freighters bound for Genoa, Italy. Three days into the cruise, a U-boat torpedoed the British ship SS *Messidor*. While another patrol boat picked up survivors from the *Messidor*, the *Venetia* searched for the U-boat, dropping depth charges. The convoy safely reached Genoa two days later.

Several more round-trip convoy escort missions in the Mediterranean followed for the *Venetia* before the armistice was signed on November 11, 1918, ending World War I. With a gold "star of reward" decorating its smokestack, the yacht steamed for the United States a month later.

As the yacht passed through the Panama Canal on February 3, the *San Diego Union* announced to its readers that "the Venetia, battle-scarred and hero of four encounters with U-boats," was bound for San Diego. When the *Union* heralded the yacht's arrival in port two weeks later, a mythology appeared to be developing. The newspaper chronicled in colorful detail the many successful combat exploits by the converted yacht, including a surprising tale of the *Venetia's* "crippling of the U-39, the German submarine that sank the Lusitania."

The story of the *Venetia's* victory over the infamous submarine that had sunk the RMS *Lusitania* would be repeated endlessly, even though *U-20*, the submarine that had actually claimed the liner on May 7, 1915, was destroyed in November 1916. John D. Spreckels cemented the myth in 1919 when he sponsored the printing of a heroic biography of his ship called *Venetia: Avenger of the Lusitania*.

The *Venetia* was decommissioned at Mare Island and returned to Spreckels on April 4, 1919. He received a government check for $76,331.83 to pay for restoration of the yacht to its prewar condition. With the refurbished interiors and new furnishings, Spreckels continued to use the *Venetia* until his death on June 7, 1926.

After Spreckels's passing, the *Venetia* was sold to a Canadian shipping merchant, James Playfair. On March 31, 1928, the yacht steamed out of San Diego Harbor for a new career on the Great Lakes. Remarkably, the *Venetia*

Scarred by wartime action, the *Venetia* (SP-431) is shown in San Francisco Bay, February 26, 1919. *Naval Historical Center.*

operated for another thirty-five years, even returning to military service with a stretch in the Royal Canadian Navy. In November 1963, the sixty-year-old yacht was towed to a small shipyard on the northeast shore of Lake Erie and dismantled for scrap.

# THE PORK CHOP EXPRESS

*We called ourselves the pork chop express. We carried meat and vegetables from Pearl Harbor all over the central Pacific...Sometimes we'd come back from an 1,800 jaunt, load up with "pork chops" and go right out again. We were so slow that almost anything could have caught up with us and sunk us.*
*—Clarence Gonzales, tuna clipper* Victoria *(YP-350)*

With the start of World War II, San Diego's prosperous tuna fishing industry found itself grounded. The tuna clippers were called home, canneries prepared to close and idle tuna fishermen contemplated a grim future.

In their new naval uniforms, tuna boat captains and officers pose in 1943. *Portuguese Historical Center.*

But two months after Pearl Harbor, on February 16, 1942, hundreds of fishermen gathered at the Naval Reserve Armory to hear a message from a retired navy officer, Commander William J. Morcott. "The Navy needs the service of your tuna clippers," Morcott told the men. "The government will either buy your ships, or lease them for the duration." Commander Morcott also had another request: "The Navy needs men to man the ships. Experienced men like yourselves…Needless to say, duty in the war zones will be hazardous. Who will volunteer?" Six hundred fishermen raised their hands.

The volunteers—mostly Portuguese, with a few Italians—were soon wearing the blue uniforms of the U.S. Navy. Officer commissions were given to the captains and sailor ratings for the crewmen. The requisitioned tuna clippers, forty-nine in all, were painted battleship gray and given YP numbers, the naval designation for yard patrol craft. Using their refrigerated fish holds, the "Yippie" boats would carry provisions and supplies of war instead of tuna.

The wooden, diesel-powered boats ranged in size from 100 to 150 feet in length. Each boat had huge freezers designed to carry as much as 280 tons of fish. Vincent Battaglia, a machinist mate on the *Prospect*, recalled that "the cargoes we were getting were already frozen, so we could really stack these tanks up with frozen food. The perfect vessel for a supply ship, perfect. Long ranges. Didn't take a lot of men."

The Yippies carried crews of about seventeen—mostly fishermen, with a handful of "regular" navy sailors added. The boats were only lightly armed. Battaglia remembered that his boat carried "just a couple of 50 caliber machine guns; we had some depth charges, one machine gun on top of the pilothouse, and one where the bait tank used to be in the back."

The depth charges were mounted on racks near the stern. The "ash cans" provided little protection against submarines and made the men uneasy. A collision astern—always a possibility at night—could blow a boat to pieces.

Between 1942 and 1945, the Yippies traveled thousands of miles, delivering supplies to naval stations throughout the war zone. The boats were slow—ten knots was the top speed—but the durable vessels were crewed by the most experienced seamen in the Pacific. The boats usually traveled in small convoys but occasionally ran singularly.

It wasn't always frozen food in the Yippie cargo holds. In June 1942, three tuna clippers at Pearl Harbor—*Victoria*, *Yankee* and *Queen Mary*—prepared to load meat and vegetables for a run to Midway Island. Captain Manuel Freitas on the *Victoria* remembered that "something unusual was up":

> *A fleet of trucks rolled down the dock and started unloading 50-gallon drums. Instead of meat and butter, they filled our fish holds with their drums. After they filled the holds and bait tanks, they piled drums up and down the deck...Just before pulling out, they told me the drums were aviation gas and be careful with cigarettes or sparks from the stack.*

The three clippers headed for Midway—1,300 miles away—with thirteen PT boats in escort. In the hot weather, the nervous crews hosed down the gas drums every two hours to minimize the chance of explosion. Reaching Midway, the fuel was quickly unloaded. "When the last drum was off the ship, an officer jumped aboard and told Freitas, 'Start steamin', skipper. Put some miles between you and Midway. This place is going to get hot!'" The pivotal Battle of Midway began the next day. The three tuna clippers had delivered critical supplies of aviation fuel that helped navy pilots find and destroy the Japanese fleet.

The steel tuna clipper *Paramount*, shown in port in 1940, served and sank in the Pacific as **YP-289**. *Lucile Madruga*.

Captain Ed Madruga had a very different mission in December 1942. In New Caledonia, the navy filled Madruga's *Paramount* and another Yippie boat, the *Picaroto*, with boxes of cans. The clippers then headed for Guadalcanal, escorted by two destroyers. The little convoy reached its destination two days before Christmas. "Our holds were filled with boxes of turkeys and potatoes and cranberry sauce and all the fixins'," Madruga remembered. "We delivered Christmas dinners to the Marines on Guadalcanal."

Under a different skipper, the *Paramount* would be lost later in the war. A transport ship, adrift in a storm, rammed the tuna boat in the stern. Exploding depth charges wrecked the transport and sank the *Paramount*. Sixteen other Yippie boats were lost in the war—sunk by enemy fire or wrecked by storms or accidents. The *Triunfo* blew up in a minefield northwest of Hawaii, killing almost its entire crew. The *Yankee* disappeared on a mission with all hands.

Other boats and crews were welcomed home as heroes after the war ended in August 1945. The *Azoreana, Victoria, Normandie* and other veterans led the tuna industry to unprecedented prosperity in the 1950s when San Diego emerged as the "Tuna Capital of the World."

PART IV

# SINS OF THE CITY

## THE LIQUOR FIXERS

*The Police Department got the liquor, fixers got the money,*
*and the Legionnaires laughed.*
*–Abraham "Abe" Sauer, editor and publisher,* San Diego Herald

In mid-August 1929, the California posts of the American Legion gathered in San Diego for its eleventh annual convention. By boat, auto and train, the "joyous, ebullient crowd of World War veterans" poured into the city, filling the streets and hotels of downtown San Diego.

The newspapers noted the "carnival spirit" brought by the conventioneers. Although prohibition was the law of the land, the legionnaires seemed to anticipate a "spirit-filled" good time in San Diego. Like most convention cities, San Diego was expected to ignore the dry laws on behalf of its visitors.

To ensure an ample supply of quality liquor, an "irrigation committee" of legionnaires approached San Diego's best-known bootlegger, Charlie Muloch, several days before the convention began. Muloch produced liquor from several local stills—from Pacific Beach to Lemon Grove—and dispensed his product from a "health clinic" on Fourth Street. Muloch agreed to supply the convention with "good, safe liquor," cementing the deal by offering to donate one dollar to the irrigation committee for each gallon sold.

*Above*: "I am not going to bother conventions," promised Police Chief Arthur Hill. *San Diego Police Museum*.

*Left*: Police officer George Churchman, head of the "police morals detail," in 1929. *San Diego Police Museum*.

Security for the operation would not be an issue. The bootleggers had approached Mayor Harry Clark and Police Chief Arthur Hill before the convention, and both officials agreed to "see, hear, and do nothing." "I know how it is when conventions come," Hill told the men. "I am not going to bother conventions, particularly the American Legion."

With the law fixed, Muloch and several associates opened a storeroom at 858 Seventh Street, not far from the convention site at the auditorium of San Diego High School. Six telephones were installed to take orders. Everything appeared to be in order. But two days before the convention opened, on Saturday night, August 17, a police vice squad raided the room on Seventh.

Chief Hill may have known of the bootlegger's plans, but no one had bothered to inform Lieutenant George Churchman, head of the police morals detail. A tip from someone "sore at the Legion" had mistakenly gone to Churchman instead of Hill. The conscientious lieutenant and his squad arrested five men at the scene and grabbed 4,500 bottles of gin and whiskey valued at $27,000.

Three days later, the American Legion closed its "largest and best" convention with resolutions lauding San Diego as a host city. Presumably, the legionnaires had found adequate alternative supplies of liquid refreshments. Vendors from Los Angeles and Tijuana had taken up the slack.

But for San Diego civic officials, the embarrassment of a "liquor fixing" scandal was only beginning. The city's three daily newspapers questioned the apparent openness of the liquor sales. Abe Sauer, editor of the weekly *Herald*, flatly stated, "Somebody paid money to somebody in return for permission to violate the law."

The city council loudly promised to study charges that "higher-ups" had protected local vice. Its inquiry would "take the stigma off many innocent officials," Councilman J.V. Alexander pledged. Police Chief Hill was directed to "lend every possible aid to the investigation."

The first serious probe of the scandal came from the county grand jury, which began grilling city officials and local legionnaires in September. Little of the jury testimony was revealed, but the newspapers reported that a local printer had testified about a leaflet printed before the convention, listing "trustworthy" telephone numbers "which the thirsty were advised to call."

The local investigation stepped aside when the federal grand jury took up the case. Sixteen San Diegans were indicted on charges of conspiracy to violate the National Prohibition Act. Surprisingly, San Diego officials were spared, but a dozen bootleggers were indicted, along with four men alleged to be the "fixers."

Charlie Muloch was the star defendant when trial began in federal court on January 20, 1930. The bootlegger described how the "irrigation committee" from the American Legion had requested his services as a single-source supplier, to protect their conventioneers from "poison liquor" from unknown vendors. Muloch had agreed to furnish good liquor at $4.50 per bottle. The committee had assured the bootlegger that there would be no interference from the authorities.

The base of operations would be the supply room on Seventh Street. Business cards were printed with the phone numbers of the room. As protection against hindrance from police, tickets called "Buddy Cards" were distributed as get-out-of-jail cards.

But then "the knock-over" came on August 17. Muloch and four others were arrested and their booze taken. The Buddy Cards "did not function as expected," Muloch lamented. When the bootleggers were taken to police headquarters at 732 Second Street, Lieutenant Churchman was standing out front. "They seemed confused and didn't know what to do."

Federal authorities had been more decisive and appropriated the liquor within hours of the knock-over. Muloch revealed that more government raids in the following days had cost him about $100,000 in lost liquor taken from his other "plants" in the city. "I do believe there were some arrangements to fix the authorities," he testified. But the protection had only been an assumption.

On January 24, the federal grand jury announced guilty verdicts for six men. Another five defendants, including Charles Muloch, had already pleaded guilty. Sentences ranged from twenty days in jail to six months.

The unindicted mayor of San Diego and his chief of police would soon be out of office. Harry Clark was defeated in a bid for reelection in April 1931. Arthur Hill would be demoted by the new mayor to the rank of captain and assigned to the traffic squad. Lieutenant Churchman retired the next year at age forty-three and drew a city pension until his death at age ninety-five.

# THE RUMRUNNERS

*San Diego, San Pedro and Santa Barbara have become the focal point of the rum runners operating on the Pacific coast…It is believed that the bulk of the rum fleet will arrive in southern California waters, literally flooding this part of the state with booze of all descriptions.*
—San Diego Union, *May 12, 1925*

The "noble experiment" of prohibition—which outlawed most manufacture, sales and transportation of intoxicating liquor—began in 1920 with the passage of the Eighteenth Amendment. An assortment of unintended consequences accompanied prohibition, including a rise in organized crime.

One example was rumrunning from America's wet neighbors—Canada and Mexico. It was perfectly legal for these countries to import and sell liquor. Canadian imports of liquor grew sixfold during prohibition; Mexican imports grew eightfold. Most of this alcohol would be smuggled into the United States, across the border and by sea.

A visible symptom of prohibition was "Rum Row." Along both the Atlantic and Pacific seaboards, scores of smuggler ships lined the coastline. These foreign-flagged "mother ships" brought tons of liquor to America, anchored in international waters (three miles offshore) and fed swarms of small "contact boats" that brought the contraband to shore.

The profits from smuggling liquor were enormous. A *Time* magazine exposé in 1925 tallied the takings: "A case at Rum Row, $25; on the beach, $40; to the retail bootlegger, $50; to the consumer, $70 or $6 a bottle."

Defending America against this wet onslaught was the U.S. Coast Guard. Undermanned and underfunded, the Coast Guard attempted to protect a six-thousand-mile coastline. The job was mostly futile at first. But between 1924 and 1926, personnel grew by 50 percent. Scores of new ships were added to the service in an attempt to match the growing number of smuggling vessels. New international agreements helped. In 1924, maritime nations agreed to recognize a "twelve-mile limit" that allowed the seizure of ships up to "one hour steaming distance" from shore.

In the summer of 1925, the Coast Guard went to war against the rumrunners. Concentrating its forces against the major smuggler fleets off the New York coast, the service managed to capture some of the fleet and scatter the rest. It was considered a major success, but only for the East Coast. The rumrunners relocated and redoubled their efforts elsewhere, particularly off the coast of Southern California.

As the Atlantic smuggler fleets declined, the Rum Row off Southern California grew. Breathless newspaper reports announced the arrival of each summer's liquor armada: "A huge rum fleet, carrying cargoes valued at several million dollars, is lying off Southern California," the *Los Angeles Times* reported in May 1925. And the following summer: "Sixteen British, Belgian, Panamanian and Mexican rum-runners, the greatest mobilization of liquor-laden ships in the history of the Pacific rum-running, are hovering off San Diego."

The usual practice was for the fleet of mother ships—the Rum Row—to anchor many miles offshore (respecting the twelve-mile limit), in locations

A notorious mother ship of the Pacific Coast rumrunners was the five-masted schooner *Malahat*. *Vancouver Maritime Museum.*

ranging from the Channel Islands to Ensenada. A popular anchorage was the shallow waters of Cortes Bank, about one hundred miles west of Point Loma.

The best-known mother ship for the rumrunners was the *Malahat*, an auxiliary-diesel, five-masted schooner from Canada. Capable of carrying as many as sixty thousand cases of liquor, the schooner would arrive in the Southland with liquor loaded in its home port of Vancouver, British Columbia.

Sometimes the *Malahat* and other big mother ships like the *Mogul*, *Principio* or *Marion Douglas* would wait along Rum Row for freights of liquor arriving from Europe, Australia, Tahiti or Mexico. The smugglers would then load smaller "intermediate" boats that moved the cargoes closer to the coast. Finally, on dark nights, speedboats arrived to whisk the illegal booze to shore and to trucks waiting on the beach.

The Coast Guard could do little but annoy the rumrunners. Its task was to watch the mother ships and intercept the movement of liquor to shore. Its only weapons were the Los Angeles–based *Vaughan*, an aging World War I sub-chaser, and the San Diego–based *Tamaroa*, an ex-tugboat so slow it was called "the sea cow."

The smuggler boats were faster than anything the Coast Guard had. Many were powered with a popular war surplus airplane engine—the four-hundred-horsepower Liberty V-12, which pushed the boats to speeds of forty knots. The workhouse engine of World War I fighter planes became the motor of choice for the rumrunners.

Shortwave radio communication linked the speedboats to the mother ships and to watchers on shore. A Coast Guard official observed, "The rum runners have perfected a system of communication that is little short of marvelous. There have been times when a fast launch loaded with liquor broke down when nearing shore. In a very short time a rescue boat would appear, the liquor would be transferred and the crippled boats would sail into port for repairs."

The local Coast Guard began to get some help in the mid-1920s. Fresh from success on the East Coast, the government transferred several fast cutters to Southern California. Ten new patrol boats armed with cannons were commissioned in San Francisco and sent south. Augmenting the Coast Guard fleet were several confiscated rumrunner boats (including a speedboat called *Skedaddle*, reportedly built for newspaper tycoon William Randolph Hearst).

While victories at sea remained few, major successes against smuggling came on land. In November 1926, federal investigators announced the breakup of a Vancouver syndicate known as the Canadian Consolidated Exporters Limited. Believed to virtually monopolize Pacific Coast rumrunning, the syndicate controlled most of the mother ships, including the flagship *Malahat*. With the syndicate exposed, Canadian authorities began their own investigations, which complicated business for the smugglers.

But the rumrunners persisted. Sightings of liquor-laden ships off Southern California's coast continued into the late 1920s. Only the repeal of prohibition in 1933 brought an end to the lucrative trade and the thirteen-year war against Rum Row.

On June 17, 1934, the *Los Angeles Times* printed an obituary for the smugglers: "The steamer Mogul, once the pride of San Diego's rum row, is now on her way home, to Vancouver, B.C., the loser in her long battle with United States customs officers and Coast Guard...Thus has California's rum row gasped its last breath."

# A GAMBLING WAR IN THE CITY

On Monday morning, July 22, 1935, San Diegans opened their morning newspaper to see a stunning headline: "AGUA CALIENTE PADLOCKED." The enormously popular resort and casino in Tijuana was closed following the order of President Lázaro Cárdenas to end gambling in Mexico.

The closing of the lavish resort sent shudders across the border. Agua Caliente had been massively profitable to the resort's American owners but also to San Diego merchants, who earned an estimated $300,000 monthly supplying goods and services. Public officials voiced concern about the end of gambling in Tijuana. Would illegal gaming now grow in San Diego? Police Chief George Sears assured the public that "the gambling lid was on."

But the "lid" was teetering. Long known as an "open town," officials often turned a blind eye to illicit activities that boosted the city's reputation as a mecca for tourists and the military. Despite occasional vice raids to clean up the town "once and for all," gambling and prostitution flourished north of the border.

San Diego was also viewed as a region where public officials could be "bought." Abe Sauer, the cynical newspaper publisher of the local *Herald*, railed weekly against officials he judged corrupt. But Sauer recognized that vice could also be means for favorable publicity, noting that "whenever a chief of police or a district attorney or a sheriff wanted to land on the front pages of the local papers he staged a gambling raid."

Sauer, then, was not surprised on October 16, 1935, when the newspapers heralded one of the biggest raids in several years. Storming a "palatial residence" near Imperial Beach, sheriff's deputies arrested several men and confiscated $15,500 worth of gambling paraphernalia that appeared remarkably similar to equipment recently used in the now closed Agua Caliente casino.

The entire house was fitted out as a casino, with each room set up for a specific game: blackjack in one room, poker or roulette in other rooms. The deputies found a large kitchen stocked with sandwiches and liquor, and rooms were decorated with antiques and hand-carved furniture. Heavy velvet drapes hung from the walls to cut down on noise.

Outside the house, a tall pole stood on a corner of the lot with a blue light on top. Visible for two miles, the light burned brightly on nights when gaming was underway. Four "owners" of the house were eventually convicted of gaming charges, with sentences ranging from ten to twenty days.

City police officers had their turn for glory on November 13 with a raid on the San Diego Club at 1250 Sixth Avenue. The police gathered up slot

The San Diego County Jail was built directly behind the courthouse at Front and C Streets in 1912. *Special Collections, San Diego Public Library.*

machines, roulette wheels and club "script." Gamblers escorted out by police included a former city councilman, a county grand juror and several prominent businessmen. Only the day before, in a luncheon speech at the U.S. Grant Hotel, County Assessor James Hervey Johnson had declared that the "tentacles of San Diego's underworld reach right up to officialdom."

The following week, Police Chief Sears threw a surprise blockade on a dozen bookmaking venues and closed several gambling clubs and "all known houses of prostitution." The Saturday night raid also stopped the biggest gaming joint in town: the Hercules Club at 752 Fifth Street. "The raid was spectacular in the extreme," reported an amused Abe Sauer. Hundreds of people watched from the sidewalk as forty-seven men were arrested and trucks were loaded up with gambling equipment.

San Diego's showy war on gambling reached a climax with a Christmastime raid on the Emerald Hills golf course in southeast San Diego. From the clubhouse, located on a hill just beyond the city's eastern limits, lookouts could spot the headlights of approaching cars. But the

SHERIFF'S AIDS MAKE SURPRISE CALL

# EQUIPMENT SEIZED; TWO MEN NABBED

### Fashionably Dressed Guests Hysterical; Officers Block Exits; Tables, Wheels, 2000 Chips Confiscated.

Emerald Hills golf course clubhouse was raided early yesterday morning by sheriff's deputies who, in the presence of about 45 guests in formal attire, seized what they described as $5500 worth of gambling equipment.

Guests, many of whom became hysterical when they found themselves surrounded by a posse of deputies and unable to find any avenue of escape, were permitted to leave only after a thorough search of the place had been made.

Two men who said they were John Dehl, 43, and Richard English, 42, were arrested on charges of operating a gambling establishment, and within a few minutes had posted $250 bail each, set by Justice Eugene Daney. They are to appear in justice court for arraignment at 10 a. m. today.

#### Situated on Hill

The clubhouse is just beyond the eastern city limits, situated on a high hill where lights of all approaching cars may be noted by lookouts.

Many times in the last eight months the district attorney's office and the sheriff's office have united

(Continued on Page 2, Col. 7)

Here are deputy sheriffs who participated in an early morning raid yesterday on fashionable Emerald Hills clubhouse. They say that the two tables in the foreground in the upper picture are used for roulette and that the one toward the rear is for blackjack. The man in the cage is Buddy Devine, leader of the raiders, and the cage is what he describes as "the payoff window." The deputies in the upper picture are, left to right, M. E. McMillan, Tony Gerhard, Devine, Chester Gracie, Manuel Smith and Carl Coover.

At Christmastime, the police raided a thriving casino set up in a golf course clubhouse. *From the* San Diego Union, *December 9, 1935.*

watchers missed the arrival of sheriff's deputies in the early morning hours of Sunday, December 8. The raiders broke in to surprise nearly one hundred men and women in formal attire, sipping champagne and playing roulette and blackjack.

Panicked women gathered up their trailing gowns and tried to flee through the doors, only to be turned back by deputies stationed at all the exits. One elderly man tried to leap from a window but was grabbed by the heels and dragged back inside. A deputy broke a kneecap as he wrestled with "a prominent local banker."

The deputies made only two arrests and allowed the rest of the gamblers to leave after taking their names. They confiscated two thousand chips, forty money bags and hundreds of dollars in cash, checks and IOUs abandoned at the gaming tables. The seized club roster resembled a social register of San Diego, with scores of well-known names.

Smaller raids came in 1936, and the year ended with Sheriff Ernest Dort declaring the county free of gambling and "clean as a bone." But more pragmatic minds were at work when the city council decided that rather than shut down all gambling, it was time for government to take its fair share of the proceeds. In November, the council members approved the licensing of "pin-marble" game machines and began collecting monthly rent from the gambling equipment. California senator Ed Fletcher followed the next year with a bill to collect income taxes from gambling, although he took pains to stress that "nothing in this act shall sanction any form of gambling which is prohibited by law."

The Agua Caliente resort never reopened. The Mexican government opened a state-run school at the site, the Instituto Tecnológico de Tijuana, in October 1939. It remains a school today, but the elegant buildings designed by Los Angeles architect Wayne McAllister have mostly disappeared.

# The Short-Lived Career of Chief Harry Raymond

In the early 1900s, few jobs were more tenuous than chief of the San Diego Police Department. The pressures of city politics kept careers short, averaging eleven months between 1927 and 1934. The tenure of Chief Harry J. Raymond was briefer than most and maybe the strangest.

Raymond became chief on June 5, 1933. With more than twenty years of police experience, largely as an investigator for the Los Angeles district attorney's office, he brought to the job a "reputation for efficiency in force management," according to the *Los Angeles Times*.

His appointment to the $300 per month job by City Manager Fred Lockwood, though, was instantly questioned. San Diegans were unhappy that Lockwood had bypassed department candidates to hire a detective from Los Angeles. The manager cited the need to reorganize the police: "It is my understanding that there are three or four cliques in the department and an outside man could break them up better than a man in the department."

Police Chief Harry J. Raymond. *San Diego Police Museum.*

There were also sensational rumors from Los Angeles of unsavory links between Raymond and the underworld. Two local attorneys claimed that Raymond had taken calls from grifters and "bunco artists," asking him to come to San Diego. But defenders of the new chief believed that he would clean out much of the "petty racketeering" thought to be growing in the city.

Within a month of his hiring, Raymond announced sweeping changes in his department. To "distribute efficiency" and place men in "more active positions," he ordered the transfers of more than one hundred police officers. The biggest staff shakeup in department history sent several veteran officers—including two former chiefs—from headquarters to substations at Ocean Beach, La Jolla and East San Diego.

In the opinion of Abe Sauer, the crusading editor of the weekly *Herald*, Raymond's changes "turned the department upside down and left it with its head in the dust and its legs kicking idly in the air." Sauer protested that "competent officers were switched from section to section until they don't know where to report for work. Everyone who was presumed to know anything was put where he couldn't be heard."

Throughout the summer of 1933, there was a drumbeat of criticism from the *San Diego Union*. The newspaper complained that police work was being politicized by Chief Raymond. An editorial cited a spiteful raid on a nightclub and the arrests of several out-of-town entertainers. It was "apparent that the raid was not a police matter but a political matter."

A "loud-mouthed squabble over a midnight glass of beer" proved to be the turning point in Chief Raymond's unpopular San Diego career. As reported by the *Union*, Raymond was a customer at the popular Hof-Brau nightclub at State and C Streets, where he ordered a beer, late on Saturday night, August 26. The beer was "served tardily," and the chief complained to the management that he was not given proper attention.

Raymond then made a phone call from the nightclub to George Sears, head of the police vice squad. A short time later, the chief met the vice squad at police headquarters, where the Sears was ordered to proceed to the Hof-Brau and to "stop dancing at 12 p.m., confiscate gambling paraphernalia, [and] make arrests of all drunken persons and anyone causing a disturbance."

Sears dutifully led his squad to the Hof-Brau at midnight. The music and dancing was stopped, slot machines were dragged outside and the nightclub was closed. James Crofton, part owner of the club, protested to Sears, demanding to know why he was being singled out. When Sears called Raymond and relayed the complaint, the chief ordered police radio patrols to close all beer halls on their beats and to make appropriate arrests.

More raids quickly came, and the police arrested nearly thirty people suspected of public drunkenness. As the police closed the Momart Café on Atlantic Street (now Pacific Highway), the owner protested. "There was a city councilman here only a few minutes ago. He told me this was a good place!"

By Monday morning, a public uproar over the police raids was front-page news. Those arrested over the weekend—including a handful of agitated attorneys and politicians—were quickly released by a justice court judge. The *Union* accused Raymond of humiliating "ordinary San Diegans" to gratify a petty grudge and demanded his resignation.

The besieged chief denied personal malice and insisted that his orders were only intended to enforce a local ordinance that prohibited dancing after midnight. But Raymond's defense was challenged by City Attorney Clinton Byers, who said that there was no closing hour specified for the dance halls and nightclubs.

"I am not going to hand in my resignation to anybody at any time," announced Raymond after a week of rumors. But City Manager Fred Lockwood had seen enough and asked for Raymond's resignation. When the chief ignored the request, Lockwood politely waited one day and then informed Raymond by letter that his services as chief of police were no longer required.

"Raymond is not the man for the police job," Lockwood said. "He has shown no executive ability. He is temperamentally unfit for the post." The ex-chief threatened action against the city council to reclaim his job but then quietly left town for Los Angeles, where he resumed an eventful career as a private investigator.

Lockwood replaced Raymond with Lieutenant John T. Peterson, a likeable former chief who had been exiled to the East San Diego substation by Chief Raymond. "Pete" Peterson served for one year, only to be replaced by George Sears, who retained the post for nearly five years.

# PART V

# ON THE BORDER

## THE HOLE IN THE FENCE

*Scores of Americans found themselves suddenly stranded in Mexico last night when the famous "hole in the fence" at the border was closed yesterday afternoon without warning...Protest was made to customs and immigration officials on duty, but the officers said they could do nothing about it.*
—San Diego Union, *December 20, 1930*

It had been there for years: a narrow hole clipped from the barbed wire fence separating San Ysidro and Tijuana. Since the late 1920s, thousands of American tourists returning from Mexico had squeezed through the opening at night, bypassing the big iron gates at the international border that closed promptly at 6:00 p.m. daily.

The fence itself had by built by the Federal Bureau of Animal Industry; it was not an immigration fence. The U.S. government was unconcerned by illegal aliens at the international border. The wire fence was there to stop cattle. Mexican steers, it seemed, often wandered across the border, sometimes carrying ticks that infected American cattle.

Most visitors to Tijuana paid little attention to the fence as they walked or drove across the border each day through Gate 1. San Diego motor coach operator Fred Sutherland did a booming business transporting people from downtown San Diego. Others came on trains from the San

The celebrated Mexicali Beer Hall in Tijuana offered tourists "the longest bar in the world." *Special Collections, University of California–San Diego.*

Diego & Arizona Railway, which ran several times a day for round-trip fares of one dollar.

Prohibition had turned Tijuana into a mecca for thirsty Americans eager to visit the cantinas on Avenida Revolución. Others were attracted to the Caliente Race Track or the casino gambling at Agua Caliente, "the most elaborate pleasure resort in North America," according to *Time* magazine. But Tijuana was strictly a daytime adventure. San Diego area churches, PTA groups, women's organizations and many politicians wanted an early-evening closure to protect public morals from the "injurious effects of wide-open towns." After Gate 1 closed at 6:00 p.m., no one was allowed to enter the United States—officially, that is.

Only a few paces east of the gate, a hole in the fence provided easy passage into the United States. Federal officials occasionally glanced at the "accidental" hole and sometimes questioned the evening entrants about their nationality or checked them for suspicious bulges in their clothing. For the most part, public use of the hole was a matter of course.

But on Friday night, December 19, 1930, scores of Americans were surprised to find the familiar gap in the "cattle fence" sealed up tight. A few scaled the fence and were grabbed for questioning by customs officials. Others retreated to Tijuana to look for hotel rooms. And some spent the night in the open, waiting for the Gate 1 to reopen at 6:00 a.m. The *San Diego Union* reported that many of the stranded were frantic women, "thinly clad and unprepared for the cool night weather."

The next day, Dr. Jan Madsen, head of the local office of the Bureau of Animal Industry, revealed that the fence had been repaired at his direction to keep out stray Mexican livestock. "It is a government fence and it is my business to see that it is kept in repair at all places at all times." Stranded Americans were not Madsen's concern. It was "a matter for the customs department, not mine," he added.

By Saturday night, several new holes had appeared in the border fence. Enterprising Mexican boys armed with flashlights earned tips by showing Americans where to enter their native country. "Among those making use of the newly-discovered openings," reported the *Union*, "were several fashionably-dressed men and women who were said to have passed the evening at Agua Caliente. In trying to squeeze through the small openings in the fence some of the plump women and fat men became entangled in the barbed wire, but quickly were extricated by friends or their guides."

In March, agriculture officials installed a turnstile in the original hole, seven feet east of the main auto gate. Made of pipes painted yellow, the turnstile turned in only one direction (north), could not be locked and was meant to be used twenty-four hours a day. The new system was immediately tested by "scores of pleased United States residents who formerly wiggled carefully through the 'hole' in the barb-wire fence." But others protested. Congressman Philip Swing from the Imperial Valley howled that the turnstile "virtually nullified the 6 p.m. closing time," which, he believed, had been rightly established to control Americans "being attracted to Tijuana gambling dens at night."

The turnstile lasted only three weeks. "Mourners who had been in the habit of 'making the hole at one' [a.m.]" watched as the turnstile "was amputated at its base and new strands of wire were stretched across the gap, thereby closing the famous hole in the fence."

In the next several months, while the Bureau of Animal Industry fought a losing battle against new holes in its fence, San Diegans began to agitate for a liberalized closing time at the border. Collector of Customs William Ellison pointed out that 1,423,751 people had crossed into Tijuana in the first three months of 1931. Clearly, the early closure was not adequate for the busiest port of entry on the U.S. border.

Extended hours finally arrived the following summer when border officials received orders from Washington, D.C., to open the gate until midnight. On Saturday night, July 9, 1932, officials counted about four thousand cars

# FENCE PLUGGED, 750 REMAIN IN MEXICO

Nearly 750 Americans were forced to remain in Mexico last night after they arrived at the border fence, after the 5 o'clock closing hour, and not only found the holes in the fence "plugged," but were confronted with Mexican police who drove them from the barrier gate.

One Mexican who loudly championed the Americans' attempts to return to their country was, with several sympathizers, loaded into a patrol wagon and delivered to the Tijana jail. American officers did not act.

Mexican authorities have decided that if Americans cannot walk into their own country after 6 o'clock in the evening, they cannot use the famous "hole in the fence." Holes in the border fence were guarded by Mexican soldiers Saturday night, on an order from Mexico City.

It was 10 o'clock Saturday night before customs inspectors at the Tijuana gateway dropped the bars and allowed some stranded American women to enter their country.

The surprise closing of the celebrated "hole in the fence" stranded hundreds of Americans in Mexico. *From the* San Diego Evening Tribune, *April 6, 1931.*

crossing the line to Mexico after 6:00 p.m. Tijuana resorts were packed as San Diegans—for the first time in years—"tasted and sipped of their new privilege—the right to cross the international border line" after dark, untroubled by the late-night prospect of the infamous hole in the fence.

# FRANK "BOOZE" BEYER AND TIJUANA

He has been called the greatest benefactor in San Ysidro history—a mining engineer turned rancher who donated land for churches and schools and built the community's first public library. Dimly remembered today as the namesake of streets and schools, Frank B. Beyer is less known as the "gambler from the owner's side of the table"—a man with a colorful career below the border who spent his last years giving back his wealth to his adopted community.

Frank Beyer was born in Norristown, Pennsylvania, in 1875. The son of a schoolteacher, Beyer graduated from the University of Pennsylvania and continued his studies at the Missouri School of Mines. As a young mining engineer, Beyer followed mining booms and rushes in Alaska, Colorado and Arizona.

When Beyer reached the booming mining camp of Tonopah, Nevada, in the early 1900s, the mechanics of mining were replaced by other interests. In 1910, the occupation of the thirty-five-year-old Beyer was listed as "roulette dealer" on the U.S. Census rolls. Four years later, the ex-mining engineer discovered his true calling as an entrepreneur of vice in the border town of Mexicali, Mexico.

Beyer partnered with two other Americans—Marvin Allen and Carl Withington—in a Mexicali nightclub called the Owl Café and Theatre. Located just below the border across from the U.S. town of Calexico, the notorious Owl prospered with gambling, liquor sales and prostitution. Mexican authorities welcomed the "ABW Syndicate," as the three partners were called, and they paid huge shares of the profits to the municipal government as license fees.

Ironically, ABW owed its success to aggressive moral activism in the United States. The Progressive movement in California, which helped shutter San Diego's notorious Stingaree District in 1912, included the Red Light Abatement Act of 1913, which closed houses of prostitution, declaring them sites of public nuisance. Along with dry laws and codes against gambling, the

Border Baron Frank "Booze" Beyer (center) visiting the racetrack at Tijuana. *From* San Diego Magazine, *September 1967.*

moral reforms created booming opportunities for "vice tourism" in the wide-open towns below the border, even before the arrival of prohibition in 1920.

The cornerstone property for the Beyer and his fellow "vice-concessionaires" would be the Owl, but their interests also included casinos in the Mexican border towns of Tijuana and Algodones. In Tijuana, the ABW realm controlled the gambling clubs of Monte Carlo, the Tivoli Bar, the Foreign Club and horse racing at the Jockey Club.

In Mexicali, the Owl drew a large share of the American tourists who crossed the border each day in the 1910s. With roulette wheels and nearly forty tables for keno, faro and poker, the casino billed itself as "the largest gambling house on the American continent." Liquor was served by ten bartenders at "the longest bar in the world." The Owl also housed the largest brothel on the border, with rooms for more than one hundred prostitutes. Beyer and his partners crafted a slogan to remind tourists that they were open 24/7: "Both night and day, across the way, you will never find closed, the Owl Café."

But despite profitable success for most of a decade, the Owl did close in 1922 after a severe fire. Rebuilt, it reopened for a time as the ABW Club. But the death of partner Carl Withington in 1925 began the decline of the syndicate's firm control over vice in Mexicali and Tijuana. New border barons such as James "Sunny Jim" Coffroth and Baron Long moved in to dominate gaming in Tijuana.

In the meantime, Frank Beyer had growing interests closer to his new home in San Ysidro, where he and his wife, Blanche, settled in 1918. In the 1920s, the Beyers ran a jewelry and pawnshop in town. They bought ranch property, bred horses and raised Guernsey cows on a dairy farm Beyer called Rancho Lechuza.

San Ysidro was, of course, conveniently close to Beyer's business activities in Tijuana. Known to all as "Booze" Beyer, he was a fixture at the racetrack, where he was usually seen in a rumpled gray suit with a black hat crumpled under his arm. He was a skilled card player. Hollywood celebrities were known to drive to Tijuana to play high-stakes faro with Beyer. Evenings were spent at the nearby Sunset Inn—another ABW property—where the music-loving Beyer tipped the orchestra two dollars after every set.

While he kept an attentive eye on his Tijuana gambling interests, Beyer also began to show a public interest in philanthropy. In May 1924, the County of San Diego was surprised to hear that "Booze" Beyer and his wife wanted to donate $7,000 to San Ysidro for a community library. Beyer promised to build and furnish the library and establish a ten-year trust fund to buy books and magazines.

The county gratefully accepted the gift and agreed to honor a few provisos from Beyer. "The conditions," reported the county librarian, "are that his name will be on the building…that it shall have a smoking room and he wants it understood from the start that there is to be no gambling in the building." Beyer also requested that copies of the *Police Gazette*, a racy magazine in the 1920s, be kept available in the reading room. The library added a spittoon for the tobacco-chewing gambler and hung portraits of Beyer and his wife.

The next year, Beyer donated funds to build a Civic Center for San Ysidro on Hall Avenue, between East and West Park. The site would be used by the San Ysidro Women's Club. In 1927, Beyer gave land and funds for the Our Lady of Mount Carmel Church. Displaying his ecumenical tastes, he also donated money to a local Protestant church.

After a long illness, Frank Beyer died at age fifty-five on November 15, 1931. "He was a splendid character, a square-shooter," his San Diego banker eulogized. "A gambler—yes, but unlike most gamblers he gave away much of his winnings. He always said, 'the rich won't miss the money and the poor need it.'"

Two streets and an elementary school bear the name of Beyer in San Ysidro today. The library that "Booze" Beyer built is now a branch of the San Diego Public Library. While the smoking room is gone and the subscription

## San Ysidro's $10,000 Library, First With Men's Smoke Room, To Be Opened Thursday Night

Bearing the distinction of being the only public library in the country which has a smoking room for men, the new library at San Ysidra, the gift of Blanch and Frank Beyer, will be dedicated formally at 8 o'clock Thursday night.

This library, which cost $10,000, has been erected facing on the main highway, and has been accepted by the county board of supervisors. In making the gift, Beyer insisted that most men want to smoke when they read, and that a separate room be set aside for them with smoking trays and other paraphernalia dear to the heart of the smoker.

At the dedication Mr. and Mrs. Beyer will make short addresses, and J. P. Coaway, secretary of the San Ysidro chamber of commerce will make the speech of acceptance. Supervisor Hornbeck will make a few remarks, and Miss Eleanor Hitt, county librarian, will have something to say. Monney Pfefferkorn, who has presented a $1500 painting to the library, will be present, as also will Miss Warren, San Diego city librarian.

The county has furnished some of the books, but Beyer has bought many others, from suggestions made to him by the county librarian. The new library will be open every night after its dedication, although the old libray was open only two nights a week.

"Booze" Beyer funded the creation of the San Ysidro Public Library but insisted on a smoking room for men. *From the* San Diego Union, *October 12, 1904.*

to the *Police Gazette* has lapsed, the San Ysidro library still boasts framed portraits of its benefactors, Frank B. and Blanche Beyer.

# THE HEIST ON THE DIKE

*Employing tactics of Chicago's gangland, and armed with a machine gun and large caliber automatics, two desperate bandits yesterday noon sent a stream of bullets into the Agua Caliente money car as it crossed the National City dike, killed the two occupants of the machine and escaped with $85,000 in cash and checks.*

–San Diego Union, *May 21, 1929*

"Big time" crime hit San Diego in 1929 with the heist of gambling receipts from Tijuana's Agua Caliente casino. News of the daring daylight robbery by "machine gun bandits" generated newspaper headlines across the country and enthralled San Diegans for weeks.

The crime occurred midday on Monday, May 20, 1929. A Cadillac coupe from the casino with two Mexican guards was traveling north on old Highway 101, carrying the Sunday revenue to banks in San Diego. Just above National City, on a raised road section called "the dike," a black Ford touring car without a windshield slipped in behind the money car.

Shooting straight ahead, two men in the Ford stopped the Cadillac by firing bullets into the tires. They jumped out of their auto and blazed away at the money car. The two guards, Nemesio Monroy and Jose Borrego, fought back but died in the gunfire. The killers opened the turtleback trunk, removed bags of cash and checks and then raced north in full view of stunned witnesses on the crowded highway.

The guards had been shot multiple times and their car riddled with bullets. The police immediately declared the crime had the earmarks of the "mob"—possibly Chicago gangsters. The county sheriff reported that a Thompson machine gun had recently been purchased by a resident of Tijuana. The police noted that the killing marked the first use of a machine gun in a San Diego crime.

The suspects' car was found quickly. In a quiet neighborhood at Edgemont and B Streets, a man mowing his lawn watched as two men in coveralls parked the black Ford across the street. Another car pulled up alongside. The three men transferred several "large bundles which looked like pillows" to the second car and then drove off.

San Diego police found that the Ford was stolen. A cheap coat of black paint had been recently brushed on. But beyond the car and crude physical descriptions of three men, the police knew nothing about the suspects or where they were headed.

The killers were nearby. Marty Colson, twenty-seven, and Lee Cochran, twenty-four, along with a third accomplice, Jerry Kearney, twenty-eight, were hiding at Kearney's rented house on Villa Terrace near Balboa Park. They had stolen nearly $86,000, but to their shock, all but $5,800 of the money was in checks—nonnegotiable and worthless to them. Kearney and Cochrane burned the checks in the backyard.

Worse, Colson had a severe bullet wound in the shoulder, apparently from return fire from the money car guards. Kearney tried to remove the bullet with a pocketknife, but when his home surgery nicked an artery, his panicked wife called a doctor. Knowing that the doctor would likely file a report with the police, Kearney and Cochran abandoned Colson and left town, leaving Mrs. Kearney to nurse Colson.

Hours later, the police raided the house and captured Colson and Kearney's wife. Police nabbed Kearney and Cochran two days later in Los Angeles. The suspects were arraigned on May 27 in San Diego, pleading

San Diego police officers inspect the bullet-riddled money car. *San Diego Police Museum.*

not guilty to charges of murder and robbery. A large crowd milled about the courthouse, excited over rumors that "underworld characters" would attempt to rescue the defendants.

But after hearing testimony from the defendants, the police and public fascination over a "gangland" aspect of the heist began to fade. Cochran and Colson admitted to carrying a machine gun, but it was never used. They had killed the guards with .38-caliber handguns. A stolen machine gun and "other artillery" had been dumped into the ocean off San Pedro by Cochran and Kearney after they fled San Diego. There was also no connection to the "mob" or organized crime. The murder defendants were career criminals with long track records of burglary, arson and grand larceny. Kearney—not implicated in the heist itself—was a small-time bootlegger.

Colson and Cochran appeared "eager to get it over with" and pleaded guilty to first-degree murder—apparently to avoid hanging at San Quentin. But as sentencing day approached, Martin Colson attempted suicide by slashing his wrists. He recovered, and then, appearing in Superior Court, he shouldered the blame for the crime, tried to exonerate his partner and begged for a death on the gallows.

On August 6, Judge Charles N. Andrews pronounced sentence on Colson and Cochrane. A moment of drama occurred when the judge addressed Colson: "Yesterday you asked me to sentence you to death. Do you now desire that I impose the death sentence?" Colson was silent at first and then stammered that he left his fate in the hands of the court. The judge "smiled faintly before sentencing him to life imprisonment." Cochran also received life in prison.

In a separate trial, Jerry Kearney was convicted of being an accessory to the money car robbery and slayings and was sentenced to one year in county jail. His wife, Agnes, never tried in court, was released from jail after a few weeks.

Robert Lee Cochran served twelve years in prison before being paroled. But his partner in the Agua Caliente heist lasted only four years behind bars. Martin Colson, who had once begged for a death sentence, tried repeatedly to escape from Folsom State Prison. His most spectacular attempt was an effort to cross a prison moat by swimming underwater using homemade diving equipment. His apparatus failed and guards pulled him out half drowned.

In July 1933, Colson's brother, Emil, tried to smuggle guns and ammunition into Folsom, hidden in kegs of nails. The brother was caught and arrested. One year later, Colson made a last, futile attempt to break out using a gun fashioned from prison shop materials. Cornered in the warden's office, Colson killed himself with his homemade pistol.

# THE REVOLUTIONARIES

*Deportation, followed by a Mexican firing squad, may be the fate of some or all of the body of potential revolutionists arrested here by United States government agents yesterday...*
—San Diego Tribune, *August 16, 1926*

On a quiet Sunday evening in August 1926, a small army of revolutionaries began to assemble east of Dulzura, just a few miles from the border with

Mexico. Led by a charismatic renegade army general, Enrique Estrada, the soldiers were poised to "liberate" Tecate and other border towns, as well as stir up national rebellion against Mexico's president, Plutarco Calles.

At age thirty-six, General Estrada was already a veteran of many years of revolutionary turmoil in Mexico. The former civil engineering student had turned to soldiering and politics after leaving school in 1910. He achieved success quickly, and by the early 1920s, he had served as governor of his home state of Zacatecas and as secretary of war. But he was on the losing side of a rebellion against President Álvaro Obregón the next year and was forced to flee to the United States.

In Los Angeles, the general began plotting a return to Mexico as the leader of his own army of revolutionaries. With fellow conspirators— including Aurelio Sepulveda, an active general on leave from the Mexican army—Estrada began collecting money and recruiting men to form a private army of insurrectionists.

To equip his soldiers, Estrada contacted San Diego hardware dealer Earle C. Parker to buy rifles, machine guns and ammunition. From his store at 615 Fifth Street, Parker ordered four hundred Springfield rifles, two Marlin machine guns and 150,000 rounds of ammunition. He also ordered four monoplanes from San Diego's Ryan Airlines, the same company that would later build Charles Lindbergh's *Spirit of St. Louis.*

The most fateful purchase was four armored trucks from a Los Angeles garage proprietor. When the local office of the Bureau of Investigation (later known as the Federal Bureau of Investigation) was tipped to a rumor of motor trucks being armored with nickel/steel plate, the agents decided to investigate. They discovered that a Mexican salesman, flush with cash, had ordered the special vehicles, claiming that they would guard gold shipments for a Mexico mining company.

At about the same time, the New York office of the bureau got wind of the large purchase of Springfield rifles from a local supplier. The order led directly to San Diego's Parker Hardware Company. Along with the evidence that someone was amassing materials for war, the agents learned from Baja informants that Enrique Estrada was actively plotting in Los Angeles.

In early August, the Springfield rifles arrived in Los Angeles and were moved into a warehouse. The bureau put the warehouse under surveillance. Other agents tracked Estrada and his conspirators, and in San Diego, Special Agent Edwin Atherton led a team that scouted the small roads that led to Mexico from San Diego's backcountry.

On Saturday evening, August 14, Estrada launched his revolution. A small caravan of trucks and cars left Los Angeles and headed south. Federal agents followed closely behind. The caravan stopped for the night in Santa Ana and then slowly drove to Oceanside and inland to Escondido. By late Sunday, they neared San Diego.

The Estrada men kept in touch with one other by telephone. As their caravan lumbered south, a car would occasionally stop for calls to the general, who had gone ahead and was monitoring the progress from a motel room in La Mesa. As soon as they left the phone booth, a federal agent trailing the caravan would pick up the phone and call Edwin Atherton, who was coordinating the Justice Department team from a room at the San Diego Hotel.

As the revolutionaries passed San Diego and headed inland, the agents guessed that the conspirators' target would be Tecate, with a possible rendezvous point above the border. Atherton's team quickly drove toward the area. Near Engineer Springs, the agents saw a canvas-covered truck on the side of the road.

The truck turned out to be one of the armor-plated vehicles commissioned in Los Angeles. The agents arrested several Mexicans with the truck and a handful of men hiding in the brush nearby. Within minutes, the rest of Estrada's army began appearing. Amazed, Atherton's men easily collected the subdued conspirators as they arrived by car or truck. General Estrada, his personal staff and hardware dealer Earle Parker were soon picked up in La Mesa.

The federal agents had captured 150 men without firing a shot. The revolutionaries were packed into an assortment of vehicles and driven to San Diego. When the county jail was found to be too small for Atherton's prizes, the convoy continued to Fort Rosecrans, where the prisoners were temporarily housed in barracks. Two days later, Marine Corps guards marched Estrada's army six miles to the base on Barnett Avenue.

"Death against the wall" was the presumed fate for any of the men deported to Mexico. But there were no extraditions. Estrada and his soldiers were put on the train to Los Angeles in September, where the entire army was indicted in federal court for violating U.S. neutrality laws.

In the trials that followed, Earle Parker was the government's star witness, providing the details of the conspiracy in return for his freedom. Sixty-two of Estrada's men pleaded guilty and testified against their former comrades. In February 1927, only Estrada and twelve others were found guilty of crimes. The general received the heaviest sentence: one year and nine months.

With the county jail too small to house General Estrada's men, the revolutionaries were housed temporarily at Fort Rosecrans. *San Diego History Center.*

Enrique Estrada served less than one year at the McNeil Island Federal Penitentiary in Puget Sound. After his release, he tried civil engineering for a short time in Los Angeles before returning to Mexico. Remarkably, Estrada decided to reenter public life. He represented Zacatecas for several years as a senator and became director general of Mexico's national railway. A city in Zacatecas was renamed General Enrique Estrada shortly after his death in 1942.

# PART VI

# DISORDERLY CONDUCT

## A RUINED WOMAN

*That man has ruined me. I am ready to die now. I did it because I did not get
justice the last time, and I was afraid I wouldn't get justice this time.*
*—Bertha Johnson, February 12, 1889*

The scandalous story of a "ruined woman" and her shocking revenge
captivated San Diegans in the fall of 1889. Bertha Johnson, an emigrant
from Sweden, was only twenty-one years old when she arrived in San Diego
in October 1888. The young woman took a job waiting tables at the New
Carleton Hotel at Third and F Streets. Petite and pretty, she quickly attracted
the eye of William Mayne, a boarder at the hotel.

Twenty-nine-year-old Billy Mayne was well known and popular in San
Diego. The rising young civil servant had studied law, had worked as a clerk
in the tax collector's and county recorder's offices and had been a bailiff in
Superior Court.

Billy offered to walk Bertha home after work one evening. She said no and
then refused to wait on him at the hotel the next day. Billy was persistent. Would
she go walking or riding with him? "No, sir," was her answer. But one night, Billy
followed her home. He entered her room and locked the door. Bertha went the
window and cried for help. Billy pulled her back. Producing a bottle, he forced a
liquid into her mouth, telling her that it "was good for a cough." Bertha felt weak

The New Carleton Hotel at Third and F Streets. *San Diego History Center.*

and "hardly able to move." Then Billy threw her on the bed and "violated her person." Afterward, he promised to kill her if she told anyone.

Another encounter came one month later. But this time Billy swore to Bertha—"on her little Swedish Bible"—that he would marry her. By June, Bertha realized that she was pregnant. For this predicament, Billy had an answer. Bertha needed to take the steamer to Tacoma, he said. He would follow on the next boat, and they would marry, just as soon as he could borrow some money from a friend.

Billy also gave her a bottle of medicine that "would relieve her of her trouble." He instructed her to go to a lodging house in Tacoma and register under an assumed name. He insisted that she go right to bed when she got there and drink the medicine immediately. It would not taste good, he warned, but she needed to drink half the bottle, and under no circumstances should she call a doctor, "no matter how badly she might feel."

The next day, Bertha summoned her courage, but instead of buying a steamer ticket, she paid a visit to the justice of the peace, William A. Sloane, who recorded her criminal complaint, alleging that William Mayne "did under promise of marriage seduce and have sexual intercourse with Bertha Johnson, an unmarried female of previous chaste character."

The case remained under wraps until mid-October, when the county grand jury announced the indictment of William Mayne for "intent to procure abortion." A second indictment soon followed, adding a charge of attempted murder by "administering carbolic acid." Evidently, the jury understood what Bertha Palmer had missed: the "medicine" Billy had given her was useful in diluted form as an antibiotic. Swallowed full-strength, it was lethal.

Trial began in Superior Court in November. Bertha Johnson spent two difficult days on the witness stand, breaking down in tears several times. "The girl is of foreign extraction and does not easily understand the questions asked," the *San Diego Union* explained, adding that the witness told a tragic story of "atrocious character" with details "unfit for publication."

When Billy Mayne took the stand, he admitted that he had sexual intercourse with Bertha Johnson several times but claimed that he had never used force. "Everything the girl swore on the stand is false. I never promised to marry her and never gave her carbolic acid."

Arguing for the prosecution, Assistant District Attorney Eugene Daney held the court in "almost breathless silence" as he described how "a simple, unsophisticated young girl" had begged Billy Mayne to save her from a life of shame. Instead, Mayne had created a nearly foolproof scenario: "An unknown girl lands in a strange city. She is found dead the next morning with a bottle half full of a 95% solution of carbolic acid beside her—a clear case of suicide and a burial in an unmarked grave."

The twelve male jurors considered the evidence for nearly three days. When their final ballot showed eight for conviction and four for acquittal, the judge released the jury and dismissed the case. The prosecutors would try again. In February 1890, with Judge John L. Campbell from San Bernardino County presiding, Bertha Johnson again took the witness stand. The *Union* noted the witness "is a slender girl, below average in height, with light hair and blue eyes." The reporter chose not to record that Bertha Johnson was now some eight months pregnant.

At midmorning on the third day of testimony, as the court settled in after a short recess, Bertha Johnson rose from her chair and walked over to the defense table, where she poured herself a glass of water from a pitcher that sat near Billy Mayne. She took a sip, started to walk away and then turned suddenly in Mayne's direction.

Aiming a .38-caliber Smith & Wesson pistol at Mayne's head, she fired three shots at near point-blank range. Mayne slumped to the floor after one bullet penetrated his neck. A newspaper reporter grabbed Johnson's arms, and the pistol fell to the floor.

The next morning, with the courtroom "jammed full of morbidly curious people," Judge Campbell handed the case to the jurors. Eleven hours later, they returned to report a deadlock. Once again, the case was dismissed.

# HER VENGEANCE.

## Bertha Johnson Shoots William Mayne in Court.

### A Tragic Denouement of a Celebrated Case.

### She Was Calm and Determined and Fired With Precision.

### A Review of the Events Leading up to the Shooting—Scenes and Incidents of the Affair.

Among the first indictments found by the Grand Jury of San Diego County last September was one accusing William Mayne of attempting to kill Bertha Johnson. Late in November last the case was commenced before Judge Pierce and a jury in Department Three of the Superior Court of this county. The trial lasted ten days and was bitterly contested between the attorneys, Assistant District Attorney Eugene Daney for the prosecution and Walter Ferral for the defense. The case terminated in a disagreement of the jury, which stood eight for conviction and four for acquittal. The case was then transferred to Department One, and set for the 10th of the present month. Judge John L. Campbell of San Bernardino exchanged benches with Judge Aitken and opened court last Monday for the second trial of the case, the same counsel appearing for the prosecution and defense respectively as in the first trial. The taking of testimony was begun Monday afternoon and terminated yesterday forenoon at 11 o'clock in an unexpected and tragic manner.

the Court and counsel an opportunity to arrange the instructions to the jury.

### The Shooting.

The recess was prolonged somewhat. The Judge, jury and attorneys had left the courtroom. Most of the spectators remained in their seats, however, and Clark Girvin and Court Reporter Meakin were in their accustomed places. The defendant, William Mayne, sat in his usual place at the table immediately in front of the Judge's desk with his right elbow resting upon the table and his head against his hand. Bertha Johnson, the complainant, sat in the place she had occupied during the trial, at the table about ten feet west and parallel with the other. The hands of the courtroom clock indicated 12 minutes past 11, when she rose from her chair and walked forward to the south end of the table occupied by Mayne, where a pitcher of ice water stood. She held a handkerchief partly wrapped about her left hand. She poured a small quantity of the water into a glass, and it was noticed that both her hands trembled violently as she did so. At this juncture Mayne turned his head slightly, observed who it was, and then settled back into his former position. She raised the glass to her mouth, but took no more than a small sip of the water. Setting the glass down she wiped her lips slightly and started back, apparently for her chair, but as she came opposite the open space between the two

*Bertha Johnson.*

tables she turned quickly to the right a few steps, which brought her directly behind Mayne. None of the numerous eye-witnesses are quite clear as to the exact spot in her movements at which she produced a weapon, but when she

*From the* San Diego Union, *February 13, 1890.*

Billy Mayne recovered from his injury and moved to Baker, Oregon, where the 1900 federal census listed his occupation as "gambler." He married and then moved to Visalia, where he died in 1921. The fate of Bertha Johnson remains a mystery.

# DEATH OF THE BUTTERFLY DANCER

A shocking mystery grabbed the attention of newspaper readers on Tuesday morning, January 16, 1923. "YOUNG WOMAN'S BODY FOUND ON BEACH," the *San Diego Union* headlined. "BODY OF PRETTY YOUNG WOMAN CAST UP ON THE WAVES" was the *San Diego Sun*'s lurid story.

A family picnicking on the beach at Torrey Pines had stumbled across a body as it lay partially covered in the sand. Barely clad in silk undergarments, the woman lay parallel to the water's edge and appeared to have drowned. Several yards down the beach, a small suitcase was found with odd clothes. Had this been an accident? Was it possibly suicide or even murder?

Police detectives identified the victim as twenty-year-old Frieda Mann, a dancer who had moved to San Diego two years before with her mother, brother and sister. The attractive "butterfly dancer" had performed solo in Los Angeles and locally and was reportedly under contract with the motion picture company Famous Players.

Mrs. Amelia Mann told police that her daughter, known as "Fritzie," had left home on Sunday afternoon. Carrying a suitcase, she had last been seen boarding a streetcar on her way to a house party in Del Mar. One hour later, Fritzie called her mother to tell her that the party would actually be at a house in La Jolla.

A postmortem examination revealed that Fritzie had indeed drowned. Her lungs were full of water but not sand, which an ocean accident might have indicated. Autopsy surgeon Dr. John J. Shea noted two other significant details. The victim bore a severe bruise above her right eye that had been inflicted before her death. Shea also noted that the dancer "was in a delicate condition." The police followed up the latter revelation by questioning "men who had been friendly with her" in recent months.

One apparently friendly contact was thirty-year-old physician Dr. Louis L. Jacobs, an army captain stationed at Camp Kearny. Upon hearing of Fritzie's death, Dr. Jacobs voluntarily approached the police and said that

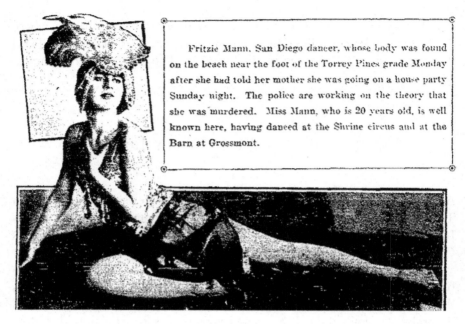

Fritzie Mann, San Diego dancer, whose body was found on the beach near the foot of the Torrey Pines grade Monday after she had told her mother she was going on a house party Sunday night. The police are working on the theory that she was murdered. Miss Mann, who is 20 years old, is well known here, having danced at the Shrine circus and at the Barn at Grossmont.

The mysterious death of young Fritzie Mann intrigued San Diegans. *From the* San Diego Union, *January 17, 1923.*

he knew the girl well. Jacobs claimed that Fritzie had been secretly married to a "motion-picture man." The doctor added that he had tried to help her get an abortion in Los Angeles but that she had backed out of the procedure. The police thanked the doctor for his information and then arrested him.

That Friday, January 19, San Diego newspapers announced the discovery of a "love cottage" in La Jolla. A girl fitting the description of Fritzie Mann had been seen in the company of a man believed to be a Hollywood movie director named Rogers Clark. The couple had registered as "Alvin Johnson and wife, L.A." at the Blue Sea Cottages at the foot of Bon Air Avenue. When shown a photograph of Clark, the motel's manager, Albert E. Kern, told police that the image bore "a remarkable resemblance" to the man he had rented a cottage to on Sunday night.

Clark was arrested in Los Angeles and hurriedly brought to San Diego by train. The director admitted knowing Fritzie Mann but claimed that he had not seen her for many weeks. After questioning, the police released Clark and announced that he had fully accounted for his whereabouts on Sunday, January 14.

With the release of Clark, suspicion returned to Dr. Jacobs, still in custody after his arrest earlier in the week. The police brought Jacobs to the Blue Sea Cottages to confront Albert Kern. The proprietor nervously acknowledged a "resemblance" to the man he had seen accompanying Fritzie Mann. Jacobs was released on writ of habeas corpus, but an indictment soon followed from the county grand jury. Held without bail in the county jail, Dr. Jacobs would now stand trial for the alleged murder of Fritzie Mann.

The sensational case drew national attention, with newspaper coverage in Chicago and New York City. The *Los Angeles Times* noted that spectators waited for hours to claim a seat in the courtroom. Others carted their own chairs to the courtroom or stood in the aisles jammed with people.

When trial began in Superior Court in late March, the prosecution argued that Fritzie Mann had either been killed or rendered unconscious before being carried to the beach. Dr. Jacob's defense team replied that with an official cause of death by drowning, there was no murder and suggested that Miss Mann had probably committed suicide.

The most effective prosecution witness appeared to be handwriting expert Milton Carlson from Los Angeles. Carlson testified that the handwriting in the motel register was identical to the writing in letters from Dr. Jacobs's own hand. Other witnesses challenged the defense theory of suicide, declaring that Miss Mann was always in "the best of spirits."

The case went to the jury on April 15. After thirty-five hours of deliberation, the jurors reported that they were "hopelessly deadlocked." Judge Spencer Marsh thanked the jurors for their service and then dismissed them. Louis Jacobs folded his hands across his chest and grinned at his attorneys. The smile faded when District Attorney Chester Kempley immediately requested a new trial.

Two months later, it began again. Familiar evidence was displayed, and testimony was recounted. But the prosecution "uncorked a sensation" when a nurse who once worked with Dr. Jacobs at Camp Kearny testified that she had seen the doctor driving from La Jolla to the hospital late on the fateful Sunday night. But another prosecution witness backfired badly when Blue Sea Cottages manager Albert Kern declared that he was now certain that Dr. Jacobs was *not* the man he had seen with Fritzie Mann.

On Monday morning, July 21, with one day of deliberation, the jury announced a verdict of "not guilty." After nearly six months in jail, Louis Jacobs, "wearing a smile of relief and elation," walked from the courtroom a free man. "I want to forget all this terrible business," the doctor told reporters. "I like to think it has been only a dream."

# THE ROYAL COACH AFFAIR

*The city council went auto buying yesterday and wound up with 20 autos, headed by a 12-cylinder Lincoln for the mayor. There was little discussion on purchase of 19 of the cars but the mayor's auto provoked much discussion.*

—San Diego Union, *November 21, 1934*

Lasting only six months, the mayoral term of Dr. Rutherford B. Irones was one of the shortest in San Diego history. It was certainly the strangest.

Irones was appointed mayor on August 2, 1934, replacing former mayor John F. Forward Jr., who had resigned with poor health. The fifty-seven-year-old Irones was a respected physician and World War I veteran. He was best known as the director of the local chapter of the Crusaders, a militant anti-prohibition organization.

Mayor Irones got off to a rough start. His first paycheck—about $100—was garnished to partially satisfy an old debt of $648. Irones recovered from the embarrassment and launched a public safe driving campaign to combat the "staggering" number of automobile accidents in the county. Pointing out that San Diego had "one of the highest casualty ratings in the nation," Irones urged the police to enforce "strict observance of traffic regulations."

In October, Irones decided to test his clout by investigating San Diego's Civil Service Commission. The commissioners supervised the appointments of more than one thousand government workers. Control of the commission meant power over the appointments. Vowing that he would "clean house from bowsprit to aft rail," the mayor demanded the resignation of every member of the commission. The plan failed when he could not secure a majority of council votes.

Irones found his next campaign more successful. He determined that he needed an official automobile. The council agreed and offered him a small eight-cylinder car. Irones countered with his own specifications: "a machine of at least 150-horsepower, with a 7-passenger body" and a "12-cylinder engine of the V-type."

On November 21, Mayor Irones took delivery of a twelve-cylinder Lincoln that cost the taxpayers $2,716. The public immediately mocked the extravagant purchase. "People are in breadlines," a letter to city council pointed out, adding that "a flivver is good enough for anyone." The newspapers named the oversized black sedan the "Royal Coach."

# CITY BUYS MAYOR 12-CYLINDER CAR OVER 3 'NO' VOTES

The city council went auto buying yesterday and wound up with 20 autos, headed by a 12-cylinder Lincoln for the mayor.

There was little discussion on purchase of 19 of the cars but the mayor's auto provoked much discussion and was bought by a 4 to 3 vote while other purchases were made unanimously.

When the council was informed that Lincolns at $2995 and $2716 and an 8-cylinder Buick at $2361.40 were offered, Councilman Warburton said he was against 12-cylinder purchases, stating he had heard protests from his constituents. Mayor Irones asked if others had heard complaints and heard no answer. A move to reject the bids was made by Councilman Rossi, seconded by Warburton, and Councilman Cameron joined.

Bennett then moved to accept the $2716 Lincoln offered by A. C. Malette and was joined by Councilman Davis, Scollin and the mayor, with Rossi, Warburton and Cameron dissenting. The car is said to carry a new car guarantee and has been run about 4000 miles.

Other purchases authorized were

Soon to be dubbed the "Royal Coach," the city purchase of a twelve-cylinder Lincoln for the mayor "provoked much discussion." *From the* San Diego Union, *November 21, 1934.*

Irones enjoyed his Lincoln for only three days. Late Friday afternoon, the mayor and his wife went out for a drive. Moments after leaving their Torrance Street home in Mission Hills, the mayor sideswiped a car as he raced up Reynard Way. The other car was knocked to the side of the road and overturned, badly injuring George and Mildred Pickett. The Royal Coach paused momentarily, then sped up and disappeared.

Two police radio prowl cars were quickly at the scene. As Mr. and Mrs. Pickett were being taken to Mercy Hospital, a young boy told the police that he had just been at the mayor's house and had seen a damaged black sedan. Patrolmen Nickel and Logan drove to the house and found the mayor walking around his official vehicle, muttering about a car that had forced him over on the wrong side of the road. "He seemed to be drunk," the police report read. "The smell of liquor was very strong on the mayor's breath and his speech was incoherent."

The mayor failed to report to work the following Monday. While he recovered in bed from "a concussion and hemorrhage," his wife fended off newsmen. "Although uninjured, she said today 'she dislikes so to make all these explanations,'" reported the *Los Angeles Times*.

Irones's alleged drunken hit and run was ignored by the police. Beyond release of the police report to the newspapers, Chief George Sears refused to comment on the incident. The city council seemed unconcerned, as well, though members did worry about who would pay for the estimated $300 in repairs to the Royal Coach. But many San Diegans were incensed by the affair. Several women's organizations, led by the influential Thursday Club, demanded the mayor's resignation for his "detrimental" conduct, which they found "particularly injurious" to the coming exposition planned for Balboa Park.

On December 22, Mayor Irones was arrested on a felony criminal complaint of leaving the scene of an accident and failing to render aid to the accident victims. The case went to trial in Superior Court in late January. A jury of ten women and two men listened to a parade of witnesses who had seen the mayor's speeding sedan strike another car.

The four-day trial ended on February 1. The jury returned a verdict in twenty-two minutes, convicting Irones of hit-and-run driving. Two weeks later, Judge G.K. Scovell sentenced the mayor to one year in the county jail. "I'll take it on the chin like a man," Irones declared. "I'm sure I haven't lost any friends...those I just thought were friends don't count."

The ex-mayor served six months and was released after agreeing to pay the hospital bills of Mr. and Mrs. Pickett. The couple later won a civil suit and collected $20,000 in damages from Irones and $10,000 from the Ford Motor Company.

The disgraced mayor, Dr. Rutherford Irones, leaving court after sentencing, February 10, 1935. *San Diego History Center*.

The doctor resumed his medical practice in San Diego, but his troubles continued. His wife, Essy, left him in 1937. Two years later, he was arrested for stabbing his twenty-eight-year-old girlfriend. Charges were dropped when the jury failed to reach a verdict. A conviction for assaulting a hotel owner cost him two months in jail in 1940. He died without survivors on February 13, 1948, at the Sawtelle Veterans Home in Los Angeles.

# THE BRIBE

*San Diego is the rottenest graft ridden city of its size on the American continent. If the Mayor and the Chief of Police don't know it they ought to be sent to a home for the feeble-minded. If they do know it, they both should be in the penitentiary.*

—*Abe Sauer, publisher,* San Diego Herald

The muckraking editor and publisher of the *San Diego Herald* was never one to mince words. A self-proclaimed expert in "the gentle art of truth telling," Abe Sauer frequently used his weekly newspaper to assault in print the political high and mighty of San Diego.

Occasionally, Sauer's attacks appeared to go too far. In a front-page editorial that he published on May 21, 1925, Sauer accused three city councilmen—Don Stewart, Virgil Bruschi and Harry Weitzel—of violating prohibition laws, protecting downtown gambling and prostitution and other unnamed crimes. The graft-ridden misdeeds of the "councilmanic combine" required immediate grand jury attention, Sauer said. He was particularly scornful of Councilman Weitzel, describing him as "the kind of man who gets his fingers full of splinters from scratching his head."

Sauer's blast drew a quick summons to testify before the county grand jury. While the newspapers speculated over the salacious details the *Herald* editor might be providing, the results of the grand jury probe surprised everyone. On July 7, the jury announced the indictment of Councilman Harry Weitzel on two counts of bribery. Charged with "agreeing to accept" money for his vote on two important local issues, Weitzel would be the first San Diego councilmen to go to trial for allegedly betraying the public trust.

Abe Sauer may have felt vindicated by the indictment, but like many San Diegans, he was cynical of the expected outcome, declaring, "We cannot question his guilt—we cannot hope for his conviction." Sauer questioned the fairness of the presiding judge in the case, George H. Cabaniss: "This judge comes from San Francisco, where graft is a pastime indulged in by everyone—bankers, preachers, politicians, and about everyone else."

When the case began in Superior Court on October 29, 1925, the star witness was not the colorful Abe Sauer but the rather less flamboyant businessman Ed Fletcher. In the previous year, Fletcher had been negotiating the possible sale of his coveted Cuyamaca Water Company to the City of San Diego. The asking price was $1.4 million. But as Fletcher revealed in court, at least one city councilmen wanted in on the deal.

"Councilman Harry K. Weitzel came to my office on Eighth Street on the morning of June 22 [1924], and asked for a private interview," Fletcher testified. The two men then walked across the street to

When respected businessman Ed Fletcher accused a city councilman of soliciting a bribe, a court indictment and public scandal followed. *Special Collections, University of California–San Diego.*

the lawn of the San Diego Public Library, where Weitzel told Fletcher that "he wanted $100,000 in advance and in consideration of that amount would dveliver his vote and that of Councilmen Stewart and Bruschi."

Instead of rejecting the offer, Fletcher suggested a conference with his business partner, banker Charles F. Stern. The meeting took place the following Sunday at Stern's office in Los Angeles. Weitzel repeated his demand, adding that he wanted an additional $4,000 to secure his vote on another council issue: the proposed annexation of East San Diego. As the three men discussed the possible arrangements, Fletcher's secretary hid in a storeroom adjoining the office, taking copious stenographic notes of the conversation.

When Stern followed Fletcher to the witness stand, he corroborated his partner's testimony in every detail. "Neither Ed Fletcher nor myself, singly or together, ever agreed with Weitzel at that time or any time to pay him a bribe," Stern declared.

A pensive Harry Weitzel sits in court between his brother Frank (left) and his attorney. *San Diego History Center.*

Councilmen Stewart and Bruschi were also called to testify. Both claimed that they had never discussed money for votes with Weitzel. On the last day of testimony, Councilman Weitzel took the stand and denied everything. "Nothing whatever was said in the conversation between Fletcher and me regarding a demand for $100,000," Weitzel declared, adding with dramatic fervor, "When he testified on the stand that I asked for money, he perjured his soul to hell!"

The jury of five women and seven men took the case on Saturday morning, November 7. After deliberating for five hours, they returned to court with a verdict of guilty. "Slumping in his chair, his face deathly white," Weitzel seemed about to collapse, reported the *San Diego Union.* His son, Frank Weitzel, who had been by his father's side throughout the trial, "put his arms around the stricken man to support him."

In the wake of the trial, the proposed sale of the Cuyamaca Water Company to San Diego was killed. Fletcher sold the system the next year

The conviction of Councilman Harry Weitzel for bribery headlined the morning
newspapers on November 8, 1925. *From the* San Diego Union.

to the La Mesa, Lemon Grove and Spring Valley Irrigation District (today's Helix Water District) for $1.1 million.

In September 1926, the district court of appeal reversed Weitzel's conviction, deciding it was not a crime for a city councilman to merely offer a bribe and became a crime only when someone agreed to the bribe. A criminal offense required a "meeting of the minds." The State Supreme Court confirmed the ruling on April 22, 1927, saying that there was "no offense in soliciting bribes unless some other person agrees to pay him the bribe."

Free but disgraced, Harry Weitzel spent his remaining years running a small neighborhood grocery store at 1209 Lincoln Avenue. He died of a stroke at age sixty-five on February 12, 1932. His obituary in the *Union* did not mention his legal troubles but did note that he had been in failing health ever since his retirement from the city council in 1925.

# DRAGSTERS ON THE BOULEVARD

*The drag street riot on El Cajon Boulevard is symptomatic of the disrespect for authority so pronounced in some areas of our society. Those who riot or endanger the public safety to enforce their demands on government and law-abiding citizens cannot be tolerated...San Diego must not be intimidated.*
*—editorial,* San Diego Union, *August 23, 1960*

It began as a mass demonstration on El Cajon Boulevard near Cherokee Avenue. Young car racing enthusiasts gathered to protest the lack of a legal drag strip in San Diego. When the protest turned into street racing, the police moved in with tear gas and batons. More than one hundred people were arrested in the bedlam that followed, known thereafter as the "El Cajon Boulevard Riot."

Drag strip racing had been growing in popularity for many years. By 1959, there were an estimated two hundred drag strips in the United States. In San Diego, racers used "the country's oldest official drag-race course"—a retired airstrip on Paradise Mesa east of National City. Construction of a new housing development closed the Paradise track in 1959.

With no official drag strips available, San Diego hot rodders used an old navy airfield near the Miramar Naval Air Station called "Hourglass Field." Automobile races sponsored by the California Sports Car Club were held on a 1.8-mile-long track. Unsponsored drag racing also took place, while the navy turned a blind eye. But when a racing accident hurt four people on August 6, 1960, the navy closed the field.

Local car clubs lobbied city and county officials for an official site for drag racing. San Diego police chief A.E. Jansen was unsympathetic, claiming that "drag strips actually stimulate highway recklessness among those viewing such contests." But one car club member cautioned, "If we don't get the strip, cars will be dragging in the streets." The warning would prove prophetic.

In mid-August, mimeographed flyers began appearing in movie drive-ins, coffee shops and car clubs announcing a "mass protest meeting" on El Cajon Boulevard, set for 1:00 a.m. on Sunday, August 21. A local disc jockey, Dick Boynton of KDEO, spread the news to radio listeners. Soon after midnight on Sunday morning, hundreds of teenagers and young adults began gathering along the boulevard.

At about 1:00 a.m. some members of the crowd blocked off the street and began racing. Between Thirty-fifth and Fortieth Streets, "cars, of all models and shapes, raced two abreast," reported the *Union*. "Thousands of spectators lined the sidewalk and center island, leaving almost no room for the cars to pass."

More than sixty-five policemen moved in at about 2:00 a.m. and ordered the demonstrators to disperse. Throwing tear gas grenades at the feet of the spectators, they waded into the crowd with their riot sticks. "Almost everyone was running toward their cars," recalled a witness. "Other people were on the ground, unable to run because of the tear gas."

About one hundred demonstrators stood their ground at a service station lot and "threw a barrage of soft drink bottles and rocks at the police." Three young men found their way into the Coca Cola bottling plant at Thirty-eighth Street. They broke open cases of Coke and began heaving glass bottles over a fence at the police.

It took three hours to quell the "mob," estimated to be three thousand people according to the *Los Angeles Times*. Two policemen were hurt, and others had their uniforms torn. A few officers lost their guns in the melee. Eighty adult demonstrators and thirty-six juveniles were arrested. The adult suspects were loaded into vehicles and driven to the city jail at 801 West Market Street, where they were booked, photographed, fingerprinted and placed in cells. The juvenile suspects were referred to the County Probation Department.

For the ID technicians in the Police Records Bureau, it was quite a night. In the early hours of Monday morning, the two techs on duty were suddenly swamped with fingerprint cards that had to be checked for warrants or prior

# S.D. Police Arrest 116 In Drag Racers' Riot

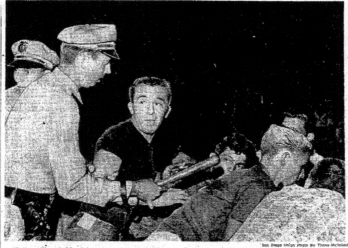

## Tear Gas Used To Break Up 3-Hour Melee

### Crowd Of 3,000 Demonstrates For Sanctioned Strip

By LEONARD ASH

Rioting among a crowd of more than 2,000 persons, mostly youths and young adults, demonstrating for a sanctioned drag race strip, was broken up by police using tear gas early yesterday on El Cajon boulevard.

Two patrolmen were injured during the three-hour melee, in which bottles, glasses and rocks were thrown at police. A total of 116 persons was arrested, including 36 juveniles.

The adults, all men, were booked in the city jail on suspicion of rioting, refusing to disperse and conspiracy. The juveniles were taken to Juvenile Hall.

**FIELD CLOSED**

The demonstration, on a section of El Cajon which the rioters had blocked off, was the aftermath of the Navy's closing of Hourglass Field near Miramar Naval Air Station to

Police officer holds club as he and second officer subdue five persons involved in riot on El Cajon boulevard. Police arrested 80 adults, 36 juveniles as 2,000 demonstrated for more than three hours.
San Diego Union Photo By Thane McIntosh

arrests through huge index name files, then classified using the FBI-approved system and, finally, searched individually in numerous drawers crammed with thousands of fingerprint cards from previous years.

Monday night brought new unrest and more fingerprint cards for the harried ID techs. Cruising in caravans in San Diego and the city of El Cajon, drag racers taunted police with games of "motorized tag." Another one hundred people were arrested. Some were charged with disorderly conduct, others with weapons charges. More than thirty juveniles were picked up for curfew violation.

On Wednesday, the twenty-fourth, the police arrested a printer named Herbert Sturdyvin, age twenty, on suspicion of conspiracy in the printing and distribution of the mimeographed flyers police blamed for the mass demonstration on Sunday. Sturdyvin was released without bail and never charged. The following weekend, San Diego police braced for new disorder rumored to be stirred from sympathizers coming from Los Angeles. The demonstrations failed to materialize.

In the wake of the riot, new demands were heard in the community for an authorized drag strip. The San Diego City Council promised to appoint a committee to "study the possibilities." The president of the National Hot Rod Association pledged help from his organization in getting an official strip but insisted that local enthusiasts would have to "reform" their conduct.

Municipal court judges dismissed most of the cases of the rioting teenagers in the following weeks. Charges of police brutality enlivened some of the court hearings. Radio DJ Dick Boynton testified that people had been struck in the head by tear gas grenades and that young teenagers were clubbed by policemen. The department vigorously denied the charges.

Eventually, the campaign for a drag strip was rewarded. The San Diego Raceway opened in Ramona in 1963 and operated for several years until it became a runway for the Ramona Airport. Carlsbad Raceway opened in 1964 and hosted drag racing until the track closed in 2004.

*Opposite, top*: From the San Diego Union, *August 22, 1960.*

*Opposite, bottom*: Police filling a van with people arrested on El Cajon Boulevard. *San Diego History Center.*

# PART VII

# FEAR AND INTOLERANCE

## THE STUDENT STRIKE

*The ruling members of the board of education are not wanted in their places anymore. The people of San Diego are not only tired of their petty politics, but disgusted with the result. The thing for those members is to slide quietly out, resign, quit. It will save a lot of trouble and expense for them to do it as quickly as possible.*
—San Diego Union, *June 7, 1918*

Politics and education mixed poorly in the spring of 1918 when the San Diego Board of Education abruptly fired nineteen teachers at San Diego High School. The action led to a mass walkout of students from the school and local newspaper headlines that rivaled news of the war in Europe.

San Diego's school superintendent that year was Duncan MacKinnon. The thirty-three-year-old, Canadian-born educator was respected and popular among students and faculty. He enjoyed considerable autonomy in the administration of the city school system. But many in the community were uncomfortable with the unmarried professor who smoked cigars in public and enjoyed dining in restaurants that served wine—this on the eve of national prohibition.

MacKinnon's tenure was threatened in April 1917 with election of three new people to the five-member board of education. The "solid three"—L.G.

Jones, John Urquhart and Laura Johns—decided to curtail the superintendent's responsibilities and adopt for themselves unprecedented personal involvement in San Diego education. The new board began by sending a questionnaire to all teachers, requesting their opinions on their jobs and stating that the recent "vote of the people indicated that certain changes in the schools" had become necessary. To the teachers, who served without tenure under one-year contracts, the questionnaire appeared threatening—almost like a loyalty oath to the board; 91 out of 94 teachers met to discuss the unusual questionnaire. They agreed to not reply individually but rather to send a collective response to the board, which included a request that the practice of tenure be considered for qualified teachers.

San Diego school superintendent Duncan MacKinnon. *Special Collections, San Diego Public Library.*

The summer passed quietly, but in the fall, the board announced that Duncan MacKinnon's term as superintendent would expire at the end of the school year. The action was immediately denounced in the community. When the board announced the imminent hiring of a new superintendent, MacKinnon quietly resigned.

Next, the board decided to limit the authority of San Diego High's principal, Arthur Gould. The principal was asked to turn in his keys to the school custodian. Board members began sitting in classrooms with pencil and notebook to monitor teachers, and the editor of the student newspaper began fielding unwanted editorial advice from the board.

As the school year neared a close, the board took a critical step, posting on June 3 "a notice to be sent to teachers whose services would not be required for the ensuing school year 1918–19." The list named nineteen teachers, including Principal Gould. Reasons for the dismissals were not offered, although the teachers were all known "friends of MacKinnon" and each had signed the collective response to the board questionnaire the previous year.

To protest the abrupt firing of several teachers, the student body of San Diego High School marched through downtown to demand satisfaction from the school board. *Special Collections, University of California–San Diego.*

The next day, a boisterous assembly of 1,800 students met in the City Stadium (Balboa) to consider action. They approved a resolution vowing to leave school and not return until the board explained the firing of the teachers. The students decided to present their resolution to the board in person. After a quick telephone call to the chief of police requesting permission to stage a parade, the students gathered in front of the school, and then, led by their senior class president, nearly the entire student body marched nine blocks through downtown to the school board offices at the Southern Title Building on Third Street.

After handing their resolution to an embarrassed secretary, the students marched back to school, picked up their books and went home. On the following Monday, twelve students showed up for class. All the teachers faithfully reported for work but for the remainder of the school year, classrooms were empty.

For the next three weeks, the student strike was headline news for San Diego's newspapers. Abe Sauer, the sharp-tongued editor of the weekly *Herald*, joined the *Union* in calling for the recall of the school board's "blundering incompetents," writing in an editorial that "their asinine work is becoming a public menace." Civic and business leaders joined the condemnation. A Citizens' Recall Committee of prominent San Diegans met with an attorney to plan recall proceedings against the board members.

The drama ratcheted higher on Sunday, June 16, when the *Union* carried a one-fourth-page paid notice from the school board. Addressed to "the Parents and Students," the notice stated the board's intention to "not in any manner recognize the insurrection and the alleged resolution of the so-called student body of the High School" and emphasized that "each and every student" would be expected in the classroom on Monday morning. But the strike continued, and a school holiday was declared for the remainder of the term.

On June 22, the *Union* published a letter from the board meant to clarify its current position. The letter began by noting that there would be no dialogue with the teachers regarding their dismissals. It ended with a stunner:

> *At the time the order was made dropping certain teachers we were informed that several among those dropped were under surveillance by the authorities for Pro-Germanism and these teachers were dropped for that reason.*

The letter was quickly reviewed by the Recall Committee, which then contacted the Justice Department and the U.S. Army. Government officials assured the committee that no teacher had been investigated for disloyalty.

San Diego High School began its fall semester on August 31 with a new principal and a new school superintendent. A few of the teachers had been reinstated, but most had found jobs elsewhere. A recall election was finally held on December 3. By a vote of more than three to one, the "solid three" were turned out of office.

# THE YOUNG COMMUNISTS

*"You can't parade. Our orders are to prevent it." In a moment there was a seething, screaming mass around the policemen. Staves and sticks began to fly.*
—San Diego Sun, *May 31, 1933*

On May 29, 1933, San Diego's city manager, Albert Goeddel, publicly warned that there was a grave possibility of a major riot in the city streets.

Scores of Communist youths and radical agitators were about to descend on the city, the manager claimed, with plans to disrupt a Memorial Day parade in downtown San Diego. But Goeddel was reassuring: "The police are ready for them."

Hints of trouble had begun days earlier when "National Youth Day" organizers requested permission to hold a parade. By a four to three vote, the city council refused to issue a permit when the students declined to promise that their rally would have no "red flags." Unperturbed, the group told the council that they would probably march anyway.

San Diego's Memorial Day parade was scheduled to begin at 10:00 a.m. on Tuesday, May 30. Serving soldiers from all military branches, veterans groups, Boy Scouts and high school military cadets, all planned to march from downtown to Balboa Park for patriotic services at the Spreckels Organ Pavilion. Automobiles would follow carrying Civil War veterans.

But the newspapers seemed most interested in reporting that several truckloads of "radicals" had arrived early that morning from Los Angeles. Singing the "Internationale," a crowd assembled at New Town Park at Columbia and F Streets (today's Pantoja Park). Several speakers—led by known "Reds" from Los Angeles Jack Olsen, twenty-two, and Jean Rand, twenty-six—took turns denouncing American imperialism and the capitalist system. President Roosevelt was attacked as a "Wall Street president" and a leader of the "boss class."

According to reporting by the *San Diego Union*, "the Communists" appeared to be mostly "children, aliens and unfortunates headed by and herded by a handful of determined organizers." Many carried banners: "All War Funds for Unemployed," "Roosevelt's New Deal: Hunger and War" and "No Curtailment of Education."

Watching the rally from the park perimeter, uniformed police and several plainclothes men seemed most offended by the banners. Sergeant Charles Glick, a burly marine, pointed out particular banners that he didn't like to a reporter for the *Sun*. "If those birds start any trouble, I'm going after those and start a collection."

After speeches and songs, Olsen suggested a march to Sixth and A Streets for a second rally at the First Congregational Church. Grabbing the banners, the crowd formed in ranks and began marching to the edge of the park. "Well, that's that!" murmured a policeman. About thirty officers barred the path and then surged into the demonstrators to grab their banners.

For fifteen minutes, the police and demonstrators pummeled one another in Pantoja Park. *San Diego Police Museum.*

Sticks pulled from the banners and staves yanked from park benches quickly became weapons for the demonstrators. For fifteen minutes, the police and demonstrators pummeled one another. The "Communists," a reporter observed, appeared to have the upper hand by the "sheer weight of their numbers." The tide turned when the police fired tear gas into the crowd.

Nine policemen were injured and sent to the hospital. The *Union* estimated that about thirty rioters had been hurt but none was hospitalized. Instead, "they were loaded into trucks by their fellow Communists and returned to Los Angeles without stopping for treatment." A dozen motorcycle patrolmen escorted the trucks to the county line at Del Mar.

Nine arrests had been made, six for misdemeanor inciting a riot. Three men were booked at the city jail for felony assault with a deadly weapon. Reports of "third degree methods" employed at the jail circulated about town, but all the demonstrators were soon released on bail.

The next morning, editorials in San Diego's rival newspapers—the *Union* and *Sun*—dueled over the causes of the violent brawl in the park. The *Union* "thoroughly approved" of the city council's decision to deny approval of a "red-flag parade" but admitted that "there could have been more intelligent handling" of the affair.

The *Sun* was less understanding. "The disgraceful riot could have been prevented by the city council," the newspaper declared. "Had the agitators been permitted to march peacefully," nothing would have happened. "Fanatical as they may be with respect to the best way of curing our social ills, these young men and women [had] the right to convene and parade."

The following week, a defensive city council sat in session and listened to a barrage of complaints from San Diegans alleging "police brutality and councilmanic intolerance." A letter read by respected businessman George W. Marston tried to strike a conciliatory tone: "We are actuated more by desire to prevent its repetition than to censure any person or group." But Marston left no doubt that he believed the councilmen were culpable, saying that it was unwise and discriminatory to refuse the parade permit. Regarding the actions of the police, Marston added, "Disinterested witnesses testify that the police, led by a sergeant of marines, charged the crowd without warning…striking indiscriminately and precipitating the violent struggle that followed."

In June, three demonstrators charged with attacking police officers went on trial. Contradictory eyewitness testimony bewildered the jury. Defense attorneys charged that the council's refusal to issue a parade permit had amounted to entrapment and that the police action had been "a deliberate and shameful frame-up."

Only one demonstrator was convicted. Frank Young, a young black man from Los Angeles, was found guilty of assaulting two policemen and given the maximum sentence of six months in jail. The leaders of the rally in New Town Park, Jack Olsen and Jean Rand, escaped prosecution, although both would appear frequently in Los Angeles newspapers in coming months for disturbing the peace in radical demonstrations.

# THE SILVER SHIRTS

*There unquestionably is a concerted move on the part of un-American and*
*radical groups to bring about the overthrow of the United States government.*
*We have endeavored to get to the bottom of all such moves.*
*—Congressman Charles Kramer, August 5, 1934*

In the summer of 1934, a Special Committee on Un-American Activities opened hearings in Los Angeles. Chaired by Representative Charles Kramer, the committee was following reports of "alarming proportions" that armed radicals called "Silver Shirts" were drilling in San Diego and preparing for revolution.

The Silver Shirts were part of a nationwide movement of anti-Communists led by right-wing activist William Dudley Pelley. Founded as the Silver Legion of America on January 31, 1934, Pelley claimed that his group would prepare "a great horde of men nationally to meet the [Communist] crisis intelligently and constructively."

Pelley greatly admired Adolf Hitler and modeled his Silver Shirts after Nazi storm troopers. His troops were "the cream, the head and the flower of our Protestant Christian manhood," Pelley proudly claimed. The men were also isolationist, pro-fascist and virulently anti-Semitic.

Membership in the organization grew rapidly, with perhaps fifteen thousand national members at its peak. Applicants were required to furnish a photograph and personal information, including "racial extraction," religion, physical disabilities, military training and personal finances. Uniforms featured "dark blue corduroys trousers, tie, leggins [*sic*], and a silver shirt with a scarlet 'L' (for loyalty) on the shoulder."

In San Diego County, Alpine resident Willard W. Kemp led the Silver Shirt Pacific Coast Division. A San Diego post headed by Charles T. Lee met at the Hotel San Diego and in an East San Diego bookstore on University Avenue.

In April 1934, "Captain" Lee was invited to address a group of veterans called the Hammer Club for its weekly luncheon at the U.S. Grant Hotel. Members were promised "an explanation of the ideals and aims of the Silver Shirt Legion."

Controversy greeted the Hammer Club the very next week when the invited speaker was Rabbi H. Cerf Strauss of Temple Beth Israel. Denouncing the Silver Shirts as "anti-American, anti-Jewish, and anti-Catholic," Rabbi Cerf accused Pelley's organization of fomenting revolutionary activities against the American government.

In his Silver Shirt uniform, William Pelley stands before his followers. *From Pelley's autobiography,* The Door to Revelation *(1939).*

It was a severe charge but was taken seriously by Congressman Charles Kramer's investigators. On August 5, 1934, the Kramer committee stunned the public by announcing that "armed men known as Silver Shirts, with secret auxiliary called Storm Troopers and avowedly organized to change the Government of the United States" were drilling in the San Diego area.

"Poppycock," declared San Diego police chief John Peterson. "There have been no drills in the city [and] the back country is calm." County Sheriff Ed Cooper seconded Peterson, adding that his men kept a close watch on the organization, which they knew met occasionally at the Willard Kemp ranch east of El Cajon. The members never drilled, the lawmen claimed, but a few members did engage in some "inconsequential" target practice.

The charges appeared more credible when the committee released testimony from two "infiltrators." A former U.S. marine, Virgil Hayes, related a chance meeting near Oceanside in April. Sitting alongside Willard Kemp on a train to San Diego, Hayes mentioned to Kemp that he was in the

U.S. Marine Corps. "Kemp told me he was the West Coast commander of the Silver Shirts. He asked me if I had access to government guns and ammunition, and when I told him I had, he made the offer."

The offer was ten dollars for rifles, fifty dollars for machine guns and twenty dollars per case for ammunition. Kemp added that any actions by the Silver Shirts would be countenanced by the San Diego sheriff's office, with the exception of the Undersheriff Oliver Sexson. The Silver Shirts would be protected, Kemp assured, but "the under-sheriff is a Jew and would be liquidated."

Hayes told Kemp that he

William Dudley Pelley. *From the* Saturday Evening Post, *May 27, 1939.*

would get the arms. Instead, he reported the encounter to his superiors, who ordered him to join the Silver Shirts. "I was made an instructor," he told the congressional committee. "I taught them the use of small arms and street fighting." Hayes's pupils were well armed with rifles, pistols and shotguns, but "mainly Springfield rifles bearing a United States Government mark."

A second marine appearing before Kramer's committee told a more chilling story. Corporal Edward Gray testified that the previous spring, the Silver Shirts had planned to "capture" San Diego City Hall:

> It was planned for early May, when the Communists were to stage a May Day celebration…200 armed, trained Silver Shirts had orders to converge on the city from the outskirts. They counted on the Communists going in before them and taking the city by storm. Then, in the confusion, the Silver Shirts were to overthrow the Communists, their avowed enemies.

The Silver Shirts' *putsch* failed when the expected Communist demonstration never appeared. A few weeks later, the Silver Shirts discovered that Corporal Gray was a spy. "Storm troops" caught the marine near C Street and Broadway and beat him, sending him to the hospital with a fractured skull.

With the public exposure of their aims and intentions, tolerance for the Silver Shirts faded quickly. The Hotel San Diego refused to allow meetings; other meeting places were closed to the group.

The national leader of the Silver Shirts lasted a while longer. In 1936, William Pelley ran for president, promising to incorporate his soldiers into the federal armed forces and do away with the Justice Department. "I'm calling in every Gentile in these prostrate United States to form with me an overwhelming juggernaut...for Christian government." Only the state of Washington permitted Pelley on the ballot; he received 1,598 votes out of nearly 700,000 ballots cast.

In July 1942, Pelley was convicted in federal court on charges of insurrection and sedition. Sentenced to fifteen years, he served ten. He died in obscurity in 1965.

# A TEXTBOOK CONTROVERSY

*The effort of the American Legion to eliminate all un-American teachings from the schools of the nation has been a real success...In fact, radical advocates of the use of the Rugg books have frankly and publicly admitted that the books are being "quietly removed from schools."*
*–R. Worth Shumaker, American Legion convention, September 19, 1942*

In the 1930s, the social science textbooks authored by Dr. Harold Rugg were standard classroom fare in schools throughout the United States. The books sold 1.3 million copies in ten years and were studied in more than five thousand school districts, including in San Diego. But late in the decade, the books came under remarkable public scrutiny and were attacked as "subversive" and "un-American."

Harold Ordway Rugg was a professor of education at Teachers College, Columbia University. The descendant of a Revolutionary War minuteman, Rugg was a respected historian, teacher and educational theorist. In 1922, he directed the creation of a social science booklet series for middle school students (grades six to eight). Six years later, he

Dr. Harold O. Rugg was a successful textbook author but a lightning rod for right-wing critics. *Rauner Special Collections Library, Dartmouth College.*

coauthored a groundbreaking book on progressive education called *The Child-Centered School: An Appraisal of the New Education.*

In 1929, the schoolbook publishers Ginn and Company began turning the work of America's best-known educator into textbooks. For secondary schools, there was a six-volume "Rugg Social Science" series; for elementary schools, there was the fourteen-volume "Man and His Changing Society" series. The books sold widely and established a model for textbook publishing that still exists.

But despite their popularity, Rugg's textbooks began to draw controversy. In 1935, a citizens' group in Washington, D.C., complained about volume 1 of the high school series, *An Introduction to American Civilization.* Calling the book "communistic," the group demanded the book's withdrawal. A school board committee investigated but rejected the demand when the members found "no mention of communism in this textbook, not even a suggestion of it."

The corporate world also complained about Dr. Rugg. When the American Federation of Advertising discovered a textbook phrase that said that "advertising costs were passed on to consumers," it accused Rugg of criticizing American selling practices by his suggestion that marketing raised the prices of consumer goods.

A national attack on the Rugg textbooks began in 1939 when magazine publisher and Hearst newspaper columnist Bertie C. Forbes charged that Rugg's textbooks were "viciously un-American." Rugg, who had once visited the Soviet Union, was also accused of being "in love with the way things are done in Russia."

In Englewood, New Jersey, where Forbes was a member of the school board, a "schoolbook trial" began, and Dr. Rugg was called on to defend his textbooks. To his relief, he found parents and teachers overwhelmingly supportive. The school board rejected Forbes's demand that the books be banned. But attacks on Dr. Rugg continued to escalate. In San Diego County, local patriotic groups and businessmen denounced the textbooks. The Daughters of the American Revolution condemned the books as subversive, and the chamber of commerce complained that they were an "indication of Communism boring from within." San Diego's superintendent of schools, Dr. Will C. Crawford, announced that a curriculum committee would study the matter.

Among local educators like Crawford, criticism of the Rugg series presented a conundrum. The textbooks had been used in San Diego for ten years and were, according to Crawford, the most nearly "complete textbooks dealing with social science available on the American market." Walter Hepner, president of San Diego State College, agreed that the books were valued for their "completeness" but allowed that he "never liked them." J.M. McDonald, superintendent of the Sweetwater school district, promised that "if any subversive matter is contained in these books they will be removed from our system."

The San Diego County Grand Jury decided to investigate the matter in 1940. In its annual report, released in mid-January 1941, the jury hit the books hard. "It was found," the report read, "that the [Rugg] books had a tendency to tear down the democratic form of government. The committee therefore recommends that the book be not used in public schools." The report added that educators "admitted that parts of the books were definitely subversive."

At least one educator took issue with the "admission." Dr. John S. Carroll, the deputy superintendent of county schools, declared that "no critic ever has brought to me a marked paragraph of the book and definitely called it subversive." But Carroll added a disclaimer: "The author may be said, at times, to express the ultra-liberal viewpoint."

In San Diego school districts, officials were quick to distance themselves from the controversy. Some responded to the grand jury report by announcing that the Rugg social science series was already being discontinued. Dr. Crawford claimed that the replacement task had been taken prior to any public comment, "not because they were subversive, but because they were too advanced for junior high school students."

Other educators loudly denied that they had ever used Rugg textbooks. Martin Perry, principal of Escondido High School for twenty-three years, said that the books "have never been used in this school since I have been here." The principal of Coronado High School declared that the books had never been used at his school "and they are not even in our library."

As sales of Rugg's textbooks declined in the early 1940s, organizations such as the American Legion congratulated themselves for their perceived role in banishing the books. The Rugg series was replaced in large measure by books authored by Stanford University professors Paul R. Hanna and Isaac James Quillen—men who were perhaps as "progressive" as Rugg yet managed to avoid the politicized attacks from the "Rugg-beaters."

# THE LAST TEMPTATION OF THE BOOK CENSORS

*This is a book of defamation, of depravity, written by an atheistic, degenerate mind—and yet it is honored with a place in Public Libraries.*
*—Jack Childres, San Diego Patriotic Society, January 1963*

Public libraries often confront efforts to censor their collections. In 1963, San Diego was among scores of libraries caught up in a bitter, nationwide campaign to remove the controversial novel *The Last Temptation of Christ* from library shelves.

The critically lauded book by Greek novelist Nikos Kazantzakis was published in 1951, but an English translation would not appear in America until 1960, three years after the author's death. Overshadowed, perhaps, by Kazantzakis's better known *Zorba the Greek*, *Last Temptation* received little attention in America until 1962, when patriotic and religious groups began calling the book "blasphemous" for its fictional portrayal of Jesus Christ.

In San Diego, an insurance agent named Jack Childres led a drive to ban the book from local libraries. Childres was chairman of the recently formed San Diego Patriotic Society, which claimed a membership of more than one thousand San Diegans. "The purpose of our society is to print the truth," Childres explained. "We believe this book is part of a Communist conspiracy to destroy the morals of our youth and undermine Christianity."

Of concern to Childres and other detractors of the novel were passages that they believed depicted Jesus as mortal and subject to temptations and desires of a "common man." They insisted that the book be removed from taxpayer-supported libraries.

City Librarian Clara Breed countered that her staff selected books based on their positive values and that library collections should reflect all sides of controversial issues. The author Kazantzakis, she pointed out, had an outstanding international reputation, and his book had been well reviewed. "We take no sides on matters concerning politics or religion," said Miss Breed, adding that "there is no record of any book ever being withdrawn from this library under pressure from any group."

In January 1963, the Patriotic Society mimeographed ten thousand leaflets, which detailed their concerns and "urged San Diegans to work to stamp out this book." Copies were sent to citizens, churches, librarians and city and county officials.

The leaflet stirred a flurry of letter writing from a troubled public. A retired attorney, Ralph Allen, demanded the removal of the book from libraries and urged that Clara Breed be fired or at least "dealt with severely." "The purpose of the Public Library is to elevate people. If a few communists and a few atheists want that book, let them buy it, but let's not make it available with tax money."

A Methodist minister also expressed alarm that the book was available in libraries. Writing to the County Board of Supervisors, Reverend Orval Butcher of the Skyline Wesleyan Church in Lemon Grove asked that "responsible authorities remove the book from public circulation on the basis that it defames the holy character of the divine son of God."

The Catholic Diocese of San Diego reacted more pragmatically. Officially, the novel was included in the church's "List of Prohibited Books" for its "salacious" characterization of the life of Christ. But the diocese declined to

Laurence Klauber, library commissioner, and Clara Breed, city librarian, turned back efforts to ban a popular book title. *Special Collections, San Diego Public Library.*

join the public protest, noting that "as soon as a book is publically condemned thousands want to buy it."

As letters and phone calls flooded San Diego's city council, City Manager Tom Fletcher asked the three-member Library Commission to consider the matter. On February 15, the commission held a public hearing in the auditorium of the Central Library on E Street. Clara Breed recalled:

> *Everyone was given an opportunity to speak. The censors were all there and included not only members of the John Birch Society but good citizens who thought they were defending morality, the church and the American way of life. Not one had read the book.*

Local printer John Kellis spoke up to say that Kazantzakis had been excommunicated by the Greek Orthodox Church for his pro-Communist writings. Not knowing that Kazantzakis had died in 1957, Kellis added, "I don't have any information that he is but I suspect the author is a member of the Communist party."

Other speakers at the hearing believed that the book had nothing to do with religious heresy or Communism. "It exalts Christ," said Sylvia Warren, the wife of a local college professor. "It shows great spiritual people have the normal temptations of human beings, and that Christ was able to conquer them."

Alvin J. Abrams, of the San Diego chapter of the American Civil Liberties Union (ACLU), urged the commission to uphold "American guarantees of freedom of speech, press, and especially freedom of religion" and to not be party to "an obnoxious form of censorship."

After listening to all the statements, library commissioner Beatrice Brenneman made a motion "that the Library Commission reaffirms our existing book selection policy and that we stand firmly beside our wise Librarian in opposition to censorship and recommend retention of the book under discussion on the library shelves." Seconding the motion was Commissioner Thomas O. Scripps, who added, "Give light and the people will find their own way."

City Manager Tom Fletcher supported the commission's decision, and the controversy soon died. Ironically, as the result of the attempt to ban the novel, library circulation of *The Last Temptation of Christ* soared. "If you really want to suppress a book," observed Laurence Klauber, president of the Library Commission, "don't mention it at all. If you want to increase its popularity, ask that it be removed from library shelves."

# PART VIII

# SAN DIEGANS TO REMEMBER

## DOUGLAS GUNN

*No man was ever more thoroughly identified with the history of a city than is Douglas Gunn with that of San Diego. No city has ever had a more sincere and zealous advocate.*
—San Diego Union, *January 12, 1888*

Among San Diego's unsung pioneers, Douglas Gunn is a man worth remembering. The onetime publisher of the *San Diego Union* was the city's first "modern" mayor and a tireless promoter of his adopted city.

Born in Ohio in 1841, Gunn was twelve when his family moved to California, where his father, Dr. Lewis C. Gunn, purchased the *Sonora Herald*. Here Gunn learned the printing trade. When the family moved to San Francisco in 1860, young Gunn worked with his father on the *San Francisco Times*, edited by Dr. Gunn. By the time the family moved to San Diego in 1868, young Gunn was an experienced newspaperman.

He purchased a small interest in the recently established *San Diego Union* and walked several miles daily from his home in Alonzo Horton's "New Town" to the *Union* office in Old Town. Gunn started as a reporter and printer but assumed editorial control of the weekly newspaper in 1871. He moved the press to New Town and on March 20, 1871, he printed the inaugural issue of the *Daily Union*, the first daily newspaper in San Diego.

Mayor Douglas Gunn was a tireless promoter of San Diego. *Special Collections, San Diego Public Library.*

Gunn bought out *Union* co-owner Edward Bushyhead in 1873 for $5,000 in cash. He quickly expanded the newspaper's size as readership thrived during a brief real estate boom, driven by belief that a railroad would soon extend to San Diego. But the railroad project collapsed amid the Panic of 1873, which plunged the nation into a severe depression that lasted for the remainder of the decade.

As the *Union* struggled to survive, Gunn did most of the local reporting and news editing by himself. The daily slowly grew and prospered in the 1880s. He sold the newspaper in August 1886 to the San Diego Union Company, managed by Colonel John R. Berry.

With his publishing responsibilities gone, Gunn devoted his time to investing in the growing city. As the editor of the *Union*, Gunn had lobbied hard for a railroad connection to San Diego. When the railroad finally arrived in 1885, the huge real estate "boom of the eighties" took off in San Diego.

Gunn bought heavily, buying several properties in downtown and the Middletown area. He built a particularly handsome building at Sixth and F Streets, called the Express Block. In a lengthy article he wrote for the *Los Angeles Times* on January 1, 1887, the retired editor boasted of San Diego's new prosperity, "built first upon the anticipation and finally the realization of railroad connection with her harbor."

Gunn's article noted that the city population had jumped from 7,500 at the start of 1886 to more than 12,000 by year's end and that new arrivals exceeded departures by 1,300 per month. The county population had more than doubled to over 35,000. But cheap land was still available, according to Gunn, and he prophesied, "The 'boom,' as it is called, will not stop while an acre remains unoccupied."

In early 1887, Gunn decided to promote San Diego to the world in a lavish book that would not only describe the region in text but also include expensive photographs to illustrate the features of the city and county. He hired a Los Angeles photographer, Herve Friend, of the American Photogravure Company. The two men traveled about the county, covering an estimated 1,200 miles while Friend photographed the wonders of San Diego County.

The *Union* described the work of its former publisher: "The illustrations will comprise natural scenery as well as prominent improvements. The process employed is almost equal to steel engraving, and the work when completed will far surpass anything ever attempted before."

Gunn's *Picturesque San Diego* appeared in October 1887. Printed in Chicago, the hardcover, ninety-seven-page book contained seventy-two photogravure plates. One thousand copies were offered for sale at ten dollars each. Reviewers from San Francisco to New York City applauded the book. A paperback version called *San Diego Illustrated*, which contained woodcut images and sold for one dollar, was released five months later. Two thousand copies of the second book were donated by Gunn to the chamber of commerce for mail distribution to the East Coast.

On the heels of this success, Gunn decided to run for city mayor. Nominally a Republican, Gunn ran for mayor on the "Citizens Non-Partisan" ticket against the "Straight Republican" candidate, John R. Berry—the same man who had followed Gunn as editor of the *Union*. After a hard-fought campaign, Gunn won the election on April 2, 1889, by 428 votes. He would serve only one two-year term. His tenure was the first under a historic city charter that established the office of mayor, as well as a two-house city council and professional police and fire departments.

By the fall of 1891, Gunn was struggling financially. Once worth an estimated $100,000 during the great boom, he had lost heavily when the bubble burst in late spring 1888. After his term as mayor, Gunn hoped to recoup his fortunes. Instead, the "financially embarrassed" civic leader borrowed heavily at ruinous interest rates.

The ruins of the Mission San Diego de Alcala in 1887, as photographed by Herve Friend for Douglas Gunn's *Picturesque San Diego*.

On November 29, 1891, the *Union* announced news that "stopped the pulse of the entire city." Fifty-year-old Douglas Gunn had been found dead in his office at 735 Sixth Street. Gunn, who had never married, was survived by his elderly parents; his brother, Chester Gunn, a county supervisor; and his sister, Anna Lee Gunn, who was married to businessman George W. Marston. He was interred at Mount Hope Cemetery, accompanied by "the largest attendance ever witnessed at a funeral in San Diego."

# ALBERT G. SPALDING

*A.G. Spalding, the well known athletic goods man, has decided to make San Diego his home, as is evidenced by the arrival of a carload of elegant furniture and a double-seated locomobile for him. Last year Mr. Spalding married a lady at the Point Loma Homestead.*
—San Diego Union, *February 23, 1901*

"Spalding" is perhaps the world's most recognized name in sporting goods. Less well-known is the man who founded the famous company: Albert Goodwill Spalding, a member of the baseball Hall of Fame, business magnate and prominent San Diegan.

Growing up in Rockford, Illinois, A.G. Spalding began playing the new sport of baseball as a teenager in the 1860s—learning the game, it is alleged, from a Civil War soldier. As a pitcher for the Boston Red Stockings in the formative years of major-league baseball, Spalding became a national sports hero. He was the first pitcher to win two hundred games and led his Boston team to four consecutive pennants. Spalding retired in 1876 at age twenty-seven, concerned—as he later told his son, Keith—that advancing age was slowing his reflexes.

Spalding's second career began when he borrowed $800 from his mother and opened a sporting goods store with his younger brother in Chicago. Selling baseballs was a hit for the A.G. Spalding and Brothers Company. The retired sports hero paid the National League to use his baseballs, which he advertised as the "official ball" of the national pastime. Prosperity soon followed as the company manufactured and sold bats and gloves, tennis rackets, basketballs, golf clubs—anything related to sport, including a lucrative annual called *Spalding's Official Baseball Guide*.

Spalding would be closely associated with baseball the rest of his life. From 1882 to 1891, he owned the Chicago White Stockings (today's Cubs) and won five pennants. Despite his experience as a ballplayer, as an owner Spalding fought early player efforts to unionize and strongly supported the "reserve clause," which bound players to one team.

Hall of Fame baseball player and prominent San Diegan Albert G. Spalding. *Bain Collection, Library of Congress.*

One of Spalding's most interesting legacies was a history commission he sponsored that researched the origins of baseball. Despite obvious links to the British games of rounders and cricket, Spalding's commission promoted the myth that baseball was invented by an American, Abner Doubleday, who it was said created the game at Cooperstown, New York, in 1839.

Spalding spent the last chapter of his life in San Diego. In July 1899, his wife, Josie, died. Within a year, he had married Elizabeth Mayer Churchill, a childhood friend from Illinois and his mistress of several years. Elizabeth was a disciple of Katherine Tingley, who ran the Point Loma community of the Theosophical Society, an institution that promoted the study of religious philosophy along with a regimen of self-improvement that included the performing arts. Elizabeth became the musical director for "Lomaland" and a member of Madame Tingley's inner circle.

While Spalding did not share his wife's enthusiasm for theosophy, San Diego did offer new business challenges and opportunities for civic involvement. The couple built a grand Victorian house on the grounds of the Theosophical Society (which still stands today on the campus of Point Loma Nazarene University), and Spalding turned his attention to San Diego.

In 1907, Spalding joined other San Diego business elites—newspaper publishers John D. Spreckels and E.W. Scripps and department store owner George W. Marston—to protect the site of Presidio Hill above Old Town, where Father Junípero Serra had founded San Diego in 1769. The men purchased the spot, where Marston would later build the Serra Museum and establish the San Diego Historical Society.

Spalding was also interested in "good roads." When San Diegans approved a bond issue in 1907 to improve local roads, Spalding was appointed to a County Highway Commission along with Spreckels and Scripps. Unfortunately, "the three millionaires" bickered among one another, and Spalding resigned.

Road development in Spalding's own neighborhood went better. He was instrumental in building roads connecting Point Loma with Ocean Beach, Roseville and San Diego, and he convinced the federal government to extend Catalina Drive (major portions of which Spalding owned) to the tip of Point Loma, now the site of Cabrillo National Monument.

One of Spalding's last acts was the creation of Spalding Park on beachfront property he owned. Hiring workmen under the direction of a Japanese landscape architect, he spent $2 million on the area he would name Sunset Cliffs. Local historian Ruth Varney wrote in her book *Beach Town*:

> *Decorative palm-thatched roofs sheltered benches where the view was spectacular. Japanese style arched-rustic bridges spanned narrow, deep clefts where the waves surged in and out endlessly...At the foot of Adair Street a path led down to two sets of cobblestone steps ending on a flat projection of rock where "Spalding's Pool" was carved into sandstone. It was about 15 by 50 feet, three feet deep at the near end, sloping to six feet where the waves at high tide broke over it and washed it clean.*

Spalding spent $2 million on the landscape architecture of the beach area he called Sunset Cliffs. *Special Collections, San Diego Public Library.*

Spalding even added a dressing room at the top of the cliff for users of the "pool." In later years, ocean tides would erode and eventually reclaim all of Spalding Park.

In August 1915, the sixty-five-year-old Spalding suffered a minor stroke. He appeared to be recovering, but on September 9, he died suddenly. An elaborate funeral service was held two days later at his home before cremation at Greenwood Cemetery.

Spalding's estate, valued at $1.2 million, was left almost entirely to his wife, Elizabeth. His son, Keith, from his marriage to Josie, challenged the will, arguing that "for several years before his death his father was not in his right mind." No less interested was Madame Tingley, who had always expected to be well treated in the will. After two years of litigation, an out-of-court settlement awarded $500,000 to Keith and $700,000 to Mrs. Spalding. Tingley and the Theosophical Society received nothing, not even after the death of Elizabeth Spalding in 1926.

# Leon de Aryan

*Shivering like a nudist in a rumble seat and leaving a trail of bayfront water behind him, C. Leon De Aryan, editor of The Broom, appeared at the police station today charging that five longshoremen had thrown him into the bay off the Municipal pier.*

–San Diego Sun, *November 24, 1936*

Public hostility rarely bothered C. Leon de Aryan. The owner and publisher of the San Diego newspaper called *The Broom* craved attention of any kind and often received it from his provocative editorials denouncing organized labor, international bankers, Communists, Jews and President Franklin D. Roosevelt.

San Diego's notorious dissenter was born in Romania in 1886. The son of a Greek father and a Polish mother, he was christened Constantine Leon Legenopol. After the death of his father, young Legenopol and his mother moved to Austria. At age nineteen, his mother placed him in an insane asylum, but he was released after doctors in Vienna diagnosed his condition as "family persecution."

Legenopol trained as a civil engineer and worked on engineering projects for the British in Egypt and India before immigrating to America in 1912. He soon joined the U.S. Army, but soldiering proved a poor career move, and after a dishonorable discharge, he fled to Mexico. He returned to the United States when World War I ended. Living in Los Angeles in 1926, he became a naturalized citizen and changed his surname to "De Aryan" to reflect his ambition to champion the philosophy of the "Aryan race."

De Aryan arrived in San Diego four years later and worked for a short time for the City of San Diego in the Public Works Department. His newspaper premiered on October 6, 1930. For the next thirty-five years, *The Broom* appeared on Monday in San Diego—its pages filled with news and editorials expounding the virtues of personal free will, vegetarianism and faith in Jesus Christ. De Aryan's columns also vented anger against labor unions, taxation and government interference in daily lives.

In 1935, De Aryan ran for mayor. As the "anti-vice candidate," he pledged to free the city from "domination by the gamblers and the brothels" and to make sure "the underworld riff-raff of the nation" would not flood San Diego during the California Pacific Exposition. Voters were unimpressed. In a race won by Percy J. Benbough, De Aryan garnered less than 1 percent of the votes cast.

The next year, the publisher's anti-union writings got him into trouble with the local longshoreman's union. Confronted at the foot of Broadway by

The notorious publisher and "crackpot" C. Leon de Aryan, photographed at the county courthouse. *San Diego History Center*.

several dockworkers, De Aryan was asked if he was the one writing articles against strikers. When he answered yes, the men pummeled De Aryan and then tossed him into the bay. Dripping wet, De Aryan marched to the local police station and filed charges.

But De Aryan's diatribes against organized labor paled in comparison to his published views on Jews. Always denying that he was anti-Semitic, De Aryan claimed that his critics were "ignorant and narrow-minded people." "I stand with the Truth" became his mantra.

De Aryan's "truth" revealed that Jews were "conspirators" who were driving the world to war in order to "plunder their dupes." He decried the "bloody exploitation carried on by International Jewish Bankers."

In September 1940, after most of Europe had fallen to Nazi Germany, De Aryan wrote, "the Jews are scuttling like cockroaches out of Europe. Their international bankers and wholesale murderers and betrayers of France are safely esconded in New York and Canada; thousands of other Jewish refugees are taking jobs from American employees." De Aryan added, "Still I do not hate them because it is against my religion."

His confrontational views drew the attention of the California Senate's Un-American Activities Committee in April 1942. Testifying in Los Angeles, De Aryan proudly told the committee he had pursued an active anti-Communist policy in *The Broom* from "practically the first issue." Because of this, he claimed, the Communists were after him and even threatened him on the telephone. Fortunately, he could identify the Reds on the telephone, explaining to the committee that all Communists have a "guttural sound" in their voices. Examining De Aryan's testimony, a government attorney concluded that the publisher was a paranoid "crackpot" who would probably savor prosecution for the sake of publicity.

That summer, as De Aryan prepared to run as a Republican candidate for Congress, a federal indictment for sedition was served by a telegraphic warrant from Los Angeles. De Aryan was booked into San Diego County Jail. Blaming his arrest on the Congress of Industrial Organizations (CIO) and Communists, De Aryan began a short-lived hunger strike but continued to publish his newspaper with the aid of friends and a sympathetic printer.

He was released after several weeks, but a new indictment brought De Aryan and twenty-seven other suspected Nazi sympathizers to Washington, D.C., where they went on trial in April 1944; all were charged by Attorney General Francis Biddle with conspiracy to break down the morale of the U.S. military.

De Aryan's fellow defendants in the "Great Sedition Trial" included several well-known American fascists such as William Dudley Pelley, Lawrence Dennis and Robert Noble. The dissidents all opposed the war and shared a loathing of organized labor, Jews, communism and President Roosevelt. A reporter noted, "Seldom have so many wild-eyed, jumpy lunatic fringe characters been assembled in one spot, within speaking, winking, and whispering distance of one another."

The indictments of the American "fascists" were popular with the public, but with no evidence to support charges that they had aided the enemy, the trial was a fiasco for the government. The defendants were unruly in court and alternately "moaned, groaned, laughed aloud, cheered and clamored." On one occasion, they wore Halloween masks. The case was never submitted to the jury and was finally dismissed in December 1945, seven months after the war ended in Europe.

De Aryan returned to San Diego and continued publication of *The Broom*. He drew public attention again in 1952 with a lawsuit to block

The masthead of De Aryan's newspaper, *The Broom. Special Collections, San Diego Public Library.*

fluoridation of the water system in San Diego. His suit failed, but voters would ultimately reject the water treatment plan. With lessening fanfare, De Aryan continued weekly publication of his newspaper until his death on December 13, 1965, at age seventy-nine.

# SCOTT O'DELL

> Island of the Blue Dolphins *began in anger, anger at the hunters who invade the mountains where I live and who slaughter everything that creeps or walks or flies.*
> —*Scott O'Dell, in* Psychology Today, *January 1968*

Writer Scott O'Dell was angry. Anxious over hunters killing wildlife near his Julian home, he needed to do something about it. He considered writing a letter to the newspapers but decided that such a letter would be unseen or easily dismissed. "So I wrote *Island of the Blue Dolphins* about a girl who kills animals and then learns reverence for all life."

O'Dell's novel of a young Indian girl abandoned on harsh San Nicholas Island in the early 1800s is also a story of courage and self-reliance. Published in 1960, *Island of the Blue Dolphins* became one of the top twenty young adult books of all time, with more than 6 million copies sold and translations in twenty-eight languages.

Its famed author was born Odell Gabriel Scott in Los Angeles in 1898. The family moved frequently, living in San Pedro, Rattlesnake Island (Terminal Island) and eventually Long Beach, where O'Dell graduated from high school. Several colleges followed, but O'Dell never earned a degree.

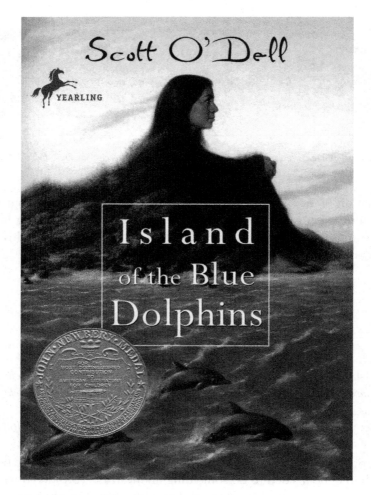

The critically acclaimed novel *Island of the Blue Dolphins* was Scott O'Dell's best-known work. *Bob and Tennie Bee Hall.*

An avid reader as a boy, O'Dell considered becoming a writer after his parents told him that he was related to the British author Sir Walter Scott (his great-grandmother's first cousin). He took up writing professionally in his early twenties by penning articles for local newspapers, where a typesetter accidentally transposed his first and last name. Scott approved of the new name and soon had it legally changed.

In the 1920s, O'Dell found writing work in the silent film industry. He critiqued movie scripts for Palmer Photoplay Company and taught a mail-order screenwriting course. At age twenty-five, he wrote his first book, *Representative Photoplays Analyzed*.

Working for Paramount Pictures as a set dresser, O'Dell had a brief role in the *The Son of the Sheik*, where his slender hand appeared as a stand-in for Rudolf Valentino's stubby fingers. He later worked for Metro-Goldwyn-Mayer as a cameraman and shot scenes of Ramon Novarro in *Ben-Hur*.

His first novel, *Woman of Spain: A Story of Old California*, appeared ten years later. Greta Garbo convinced MGM to buy the screen rights to the book. The book was never filmed, but sale of the rights supported O'Dell through the Great Depression.

After a brief stint in the U.S. Army Air Force during World War II, O'Dell joined the Coast Guard Auxiliary. He finished the war doing night patrol duty off the Southern California coast, sometimes alongside fellow volunteer Humphrey Bogart.

O'Dell was fascinated by California history and used the Mexican-American War as inspiration for his second novel, *Hill of the Hawk*. A review in *Westways* magazine called O'Dell's work "an usually fine historical novel" and praised his lively description of the Battle of San Pasqual.

After a stint as book review editor for the *Los Angeles Daily News*, O'Dell began writing historical works full time. *Country of the Sun: Southern California, an Informal Guide* appeared in 1957. Tracing the history of the region, O'Dell wrote a particularly descriptive account of the 1870s gold rush in Julian, a community where he was then living.

The O'Dell home in Julian was a remodeled packinghouse, with three-foot-thick stone walls, set in an apple orchard called Stoneapple Farm. With his wife, Dorsa, O'Dell grew apples and explored story ideas, usually based on incidents in California history.

From his research for *Country of the Sun*, O'Dell had discovered the true story of the "Lost Woman of San Nicholas," a Native American who had lived alone for eighteen years on California's most isolated Channel Island. She had been abandoned on the island in 1835 when the indigenous Nicoleño Indians moved to the mainland. Reportedly, she had jumped from the ship that carried her people to the coast. She was found in 1853 and brought to the Santa Barbara Mission, where she died a short time later.

Scott O'Dell's fictional reconstruction of the life of the abandoned "Karana" on the Island of the Blue Dolphins was an instant classic. The well-reviewed novel sold widely and was frequently adopted for classroom use in schools. In 1961, it won the prestigious John Newbery Medal for the most distinguished contribution to literature for children.

The book's success made the Julian writer a celebrity. O'Dell traveled throughout California, speaking to school assemblies and classes. In early 1963, O'Dell estimated that had spoken to forty thousand children in two years. A film version of the story appeared in 1964, starring George Kennedy and Celia Kaye as Karana.

O'Dell, who would stick to writing for young adults for the rest of his career, had discovered the rewards of writing for the young. In 1968, he commented that with the publication of adult books, the author could expect to hear "most from his friends and none from his enemies." Afterward, "there is silence." "But with children, if they like your book, the reverse is true. They respond in numbers, by the thousands of letters, over an indefinite period of time."

The celebrated author Scott O'Dell. *Bob and Tennie Bee Hall.*

After the *Island of Blue Dolphins*, O'Dell wrote nearly thirty more popular and critically esteemed novels for young readers. He spent his last years in Westchester County, New York, before his death at age ninety-one in 1989. His ashes were scattered in the ocean off La Jolla.

# DONAL HORD

One of America's greatest artists left an impressive legacy in San Diego. Donal Hord, best known for his monumental stone figures, created works of sculpture that have endured at sites throughout our region.

The artist was born as Donald Horr in Prentice, Wisconsin, in 1902. His parents divorced when he was only seven; the unhappy mother supposedly

Donal Hord carving hard diorite stone with an air hammer to create *Spring Stirring. Special Collections, San Diego Public Library.*

renamed her son to spite the father by moving the last *d* from his first name and adding to his last name.

Donal and his mother moved to Seattle in 1914. Here Donal began to display an interest in art by taking lessons in watercolors and carving his first small pieces of sculpture. The young artist was sickly as a child, and a bout with rheumatic fever at age twelve left him with a weakened heart. After a doctor recommended a warmer climate, mother and son boarded a steamship for San Diego.

Attending high school was difficult for Donal because of his poor health. However, he was a regular visitor to the San Diego Public Library, where "he was always underfoot," recalled a librarian. A voracious reader, Hord checked out books by the armload. Years later, he would show his gratitude to the library by donating his large personal collection of books and many works of art.

At age fifteen, Hord began taking art classes from Anna Valentien at the San Diego Evening High School. Valentien was a notable figure in San Diego's blossoming arts and crafts movement. She had also studied sculpture with Auguste Rodin in Paris. From Valentien, Hord began learning the rudiments of modeling and sculpture.

Hord continued his education in the 1920s, aided by grants and scholarships. He learned bronze casting at the Santa Barbara School of Arts and spent eleven months in Mexico studying ancient and modern forms of Native American art that would strongly influence his own personal artistic style.

Most of his early work was in bronzes, which required clay modeling and then casting. The process was frustrating at times; a bad cast could ruin weeks or months of work. Hord came to prefer direct mediums such as hardwood or stone. He was particularly fascinated by materials used by ancient sculptors, who had carved their work directly on the materials. Diorite, for example, was a favorite hard stone used in Middle Eastern civilizations such as Egypt, Babylonia and Assyria. A famed work in diorite extant today is the Code of Hammurabi, inscribed on a seven-foot pillar in about 1790 BCE.

Hord once explained to a newspaper reporter that he chose hard mediums because "they were such beautiful materials." Sculpting in hardwoods such as rosewood or lignum vitae or rocklike diorite or jade was difficult. "In fact, I would much rather have used something easier to cut," he admitted. But hard surfaces could be worked with precision and took a finish that was beautiful to touch as well as sight.

In 1934, Hord was accepted to the Depression-era Federal Art Project and given a salary of seventy-five dollars per month. The opportunity to carve in stone followed. For *La Tehuana*, a patio fountain in the courtyard of the House of Hospitality in Balboa Park, Hord used Indiana limestone to create the figure of a Native American woman pouring water from an olla.

It took Hord and his assistant, Homer Dana, ten weeks to complete *La Tehauna*. Hord thought that he could do his next project in twenty weeks. But *Aztec* took fourteen months. It was his first experience with diorite, an extremely hard stone. "I learned, by blister, bruise and dark despair," Hord said, "that diorite is a wonderful medium to instill discipline."

*Aztec*, which became the iconic "Montezuma" on the campus of San Diego State College, was carved from a two-and-a-half-ton block of black diorite quarried near Escondido. After months of hard work with hand tools, a quarryman suggested the work would go a lot faster with an air hammer. Homer Dana remembered, "We picked a service station air compressor, and used it for years and years."

Hord's next major project would be *Guardian of the Waters*. Working from a thirty-ton block of gray diorite quarried near Lakeside, Hord supervised a team that began by trimming off huge one-hundred-pound slabs. "I stayed

The monumental *Guardian of the Waters* stands in front of the San Diego County Administration Building. *Special Collections, San Diego Public Library.*

off of it," Hord recalled, "until we got to the air hammer and then I started in to work."

The thirteen-foot-tall statue of a woman holding an olla of water on her shoulder was mounted on a ten-foot base decorated with a mosaic of 200,000 pieces. After two years of work, it was moved into place on the harbor side of the Civic Center—today's County Administration Building—and dedicated on June 10, 1939.

Another recognizable Hord sculpture, passed by thousands of people daily, is a set of bas-reliefs flanking the entry doors to the Central Library at 820 E Street. Integrating sculpture with architecture, the two "literature" panels— ten feet high and six feet wide—represent the heritage of reading brought from the cultures of east and west.

The bas-reliefs were a return for Hord to the molds and castings of his early career. In his backyard studio in Pacific Beach, the panels were first sketched and made as small clay models. Larger, full-scale clay models came next, created in a wooden frame. Plaster molds were then made from the clay, which held the casting concrete for the final work. Cranes lifted the panels into place on the library's exterior on September 3, 1953, several months before the new building opened to the public.

That same year, Hord arranged for the donation to the library of *West Wind*, a graceful piece carved from Mexican rosewood. The forty-five-inch sculpture is on permanent exhibit in the Wangenheim Collection of the Central Library.

Hord's last monumental sculpture, *Morning*, stands in Embarcadero Marina Park near Seaport Village. The six-foot, three-inch-tall work in black diorite was begun in 1951 but took five years to complete. In fragile health, Hord returned to working with simpler materials: bronzes and terra cotta. But he would continue remarkable productivity, completing one or two major works every year until his death from heart disease at age sixty-three in 1966.

# SOURCES

## A FRONTIER PORT BECOMES A CITY

### *The Horton House*

District Court. *Patrick v. Horton. Case Files, Civil and Criminal.* Case 324a (1877).

*The Golden Era* 38 (September 1888).

MacPhail, Elizabeth C. *The Story of New San Diego and of Its Founder Alonzo E. Horton.* San Diego, CA: San Diego Historical Society, 1979.

*San Diego Bulletin.*

*San Diego Union.*

Smythe, William E. *History of San Diego, 1542–1908.* San Diego, CA: History Company, 1908.

### *Cable Cars in San Diego*

Dodge, Richard V. *Rails of the Silver Gate: The Spreckels San Diego Empire.* San Marino, CA: Golden West Books, 1960.

Eisler, Ken. "San Diego's Cable-Car Days." *San Diego and Point Magazine* (January 1957).

Haga, Susan. "San Diego's Cable Railway." *Journal of San Diego History* 15 (Spring 1969).

Hensley, Herbert C. "Early San Diego: Reminiscences of Early Days and People." Undated typescript. Special Collections, San Diego Public Library, San Diego, California.

*San Diego Union.*

Smythe, William E. *History of San Diego, 1542–1908.* San Diego, CA: History Company, 1908.

## The Carnegie Library

Koch, Theodore W. *A Book of Carnegie Libraries.* New York: H.W. Wilson, 1917.

Reilly, Karen E. "The Place of the San Diego Public Library Carnegie Building in American Library History: A Case Study in Library Design and Shifting Values." Master's thesis, University of California, Los Angeles, 2002.

*San Diego Evening Tribune.*

San Diego Public Library Papers. Special Collections. San Diego Public Library, San Diego, California.

*San Diego Union.*

## The San Diego Baths

Brown, Goodwin. "The System of Public Bath." *Current Literature* 29 (August 1900).

*The Literary Digest* 47. "Americanization by Bath" (August 23, 1913).

*San Diego Union.*

## San Diego State's First Year

Lesley, Lewis Burt. "San Diego State College: The First Fifty Years, 1897–1947." San Diego, CA: San Diego State College, 1947.

*Los Angeles Times.*

*San Diego Union.*

Starr, Raymond. *San Diego State University: A History in Word and Image.* San Diego, CA: San Diego State University, 1995.

# CIVIC PRIDE

## The 1890 Federal Census

Blake, Kevin. "'First in the Path of the Firemen': The Fate of the 1890 Census." *Prologue* 28 (Spring 1996).
*Los Angeles Times.*
*San Diego Union.*
U.S. Census Bureau. "Census of Population and Housing, 1890 Census." www.census.gov/prod/www/abs/decennial/1890.html.

## The Great Race

Fletcher, Ed. *Memoirs of Ed Fletcher.* San Diego, CA: Pioneer Printers, 1952.
*San Diego Evening Tribune.*
*San Diego Union.*

## Wonderland

Heilbron, Carl H. *History of San Diego County.* San Diego, CA: San Diego Press Club, 1936.
Held, Ruth Varney. *Beach Town: Early Days in Ocean Beach.* San Diego, CA: Held, 1975.
*San Diego Evening Tribune.*
*San Diego Union.*
Wegeforth, Harry Milton. *It Began with a Roar: The Story of San Diego's World-Famed Zoo.* San Diego, CA: printed by Pioneer Printers, 1953.

## Babe Ruth in San Diego

Cabral, Rick. "Bustin' Babes—Larrupin' Lous: Barnstorming America in 1927." The Pitchbook. http://www.thepitchbook.com/Bustin%27-Babes-Lous-Barnstorming-1927.html.
Montville, Leigh. *The Big Bam: The Life and Times of Babe Ruth.* New York: Doubleday, 2006.

*San Diego Evening Tribune.*
*San Diego Sun.*
*San Diego Union.*
Wagenheim, Kal. *Babe Ruth: His Life and Legend.* New York: Praeger
    Publishers, 1974.

## The "Stolen" Cabrillo Statue

Fletcher, Ed. *Memoirs of Ed Fletcher.* San Diego, CA: Pioneer Printers, 1952.
Holland, F. Ross. "The Origin and Development of Cabrillo National
    Monument." *Eighth Annual Cabrillo Festival Historic Seminar* 1, no. 8 (1980).
*Los Angeles Times.*
*San Diego Union.*

# SAN DIEGO AT WAR

## San Diego's Warship

Albert, George J., Captain. "The U.S.S. San Diego and the California Naval
    Militia." California State Military Museum. www.militarymuseum.org/
    USSSanDiego.html.
Kettner, William. *Why It Was Done and How.* Compiled by Mary B. Steyle.
    San Diego, CA: Frye & Smith, 1923.
Linder, Bruce. *San Diego's Navy: An Illustrated History.* Annapolis, MD: Naval
    Institute Press, 2001.
*San Diego Union.*

## The German Raider

Grover, David H., Commodore. "Bully of the Pacific Mixes It Up With
    Huns." *Traditions* (Summer 1997).
Linder, Bruce. *San Diego's Navy: An Illustrated History.* Annapolis, MD: Naval
    Institute Press, 2001.

*Los Angeles Times.*

*San Diego Sun.*

*San Diego Union.*

Shor, Elizabeth Noble. *Scripps Institution of Oceanography: Probing the Oceans, 1936–1976*. San Diego, CA: Tofua Press, 1978.

## The Navy Swimming Pool in Balboa Park

Goodhue, Bertram, and Carleton Winslow. *The Architecture and Gardens of the San Diego Exposition*. San Francisco, CA: Paul Elder & Company, 1916.

San Diego Board of Park Commissioners. "Report on History and Activities of the Naval Training Camp at San Diego, Cal." May 8, 1917. Special Collections, San Diego Public Library.

*San Diego Union.*

Sessions, Kate. "Care of Pools and Water Lilies." *California Garden* (February 1927).

## Spreckels's Yacht

Adams, H. Austin. *The Man John D. Spreckels*. San Diego, CA: Frye & Smith, 1924.

Bowling Green State University. Great Lakes Vessels Online Index. http://ul.bgsu.edu/cgi-bin/xvsl2.cgi.

Gockel, Paul W. "John D. Spreckels' Venetia." *Mains'l Haul* (Summer–Fall 2004). San Diego Maritime Museum.

*Los Angeles Times.*

Mooney, James L., ed. *Dictionary of American Naval Fighting Ships*. Washington, D.C.: Naval Historical Center, Department of the Navy, 1981.

*New York Times.*

*San Diego Union.*

## The Pork Chop Express

Battaglia, Vincent. Oral history interview, March 3, 1991. San Diego History Center.

*San Diego Evening Tribune.*

*San Diego Union.*

Shapiro, Daniel M. "The 'Pork Chop Express': San Diego's Tuna Fleet, 1942–1945." Master's thesis, University of San Diego, 1993.

# SINS OF THE CITY

## *The Liquor Fixers*

Castanien, Pliny. *To Protect and Serve: A History of the San Diego Police Department and Its Chiefs, 1889–1989.* San Diego, CA: San Diego Historical Society, 1993.
*Los Angeles Times.*
*San Diego Herald.*
*San Diego Union.*

## *The Rumrunners*

Canney, Donald J. "Rum War: The U.S. Coast Guard and Prohibition." U.S. Coast Guard, June 2000. www.uscg.mil.
*Los Angeles Times.*
MacMullen, Jerry. *They Came by Sea: A Pictorial History of San Diego Bay.* Los Angeles, CA: W. Ritchie Press, 1969.
*San Diego Union.*
*Time.* "The War" (May 25, 1925).
Vancouver Maritime Museum. "Malahat." www.vancouvermaritimemuseum.com/page219.htm.

## *A Gambling War in the City*

Castanien, Pliny. *To Protect and Serve: A History of the San Diego Police Department and Its Chiefs, 1889–1989.* San Diego, CA: San Diego Historical Society, 1993.
*Los Angeles Times.*
*San Diego Evening Tribune.*

*San Diego Herald.*
*San Diego Union.*


## The Short-Lived Career of Chief Harry Raymond

Castanien, Pliny. *To Protect and Serve: A History of the San Diego Police Department and Its Chiefs, 1889–1989.* San Diego, CA: San Diego Historical Society, 1993.
*Los Angeles Times.* June 1933.
*San Diego Herald.* August 31, 1933.
*San Diego Union.* June–September, 1933.

# ON THE BORDER


## The Hole in the Fence

Ganster, Paul, and David Lorey. *The U.S.-Mexican Border into the Twenty-first Century.* 2nd ed. New York: Rowland and Littlefield, 2008.
*Los Angeles Times.*
Profitt, T.D., III. *Tijuana: The History of a Mexican Metropolis.* San Diego, CA: San Diego State University Press, 1994.
*San Diego Union.*

## Frank "Booze" Beyer and Tijuana

*California of the South: A History.* Chicago: S.J. Clark Publishing Company, 1933.
*Los Angeles Times.*
*San Diego Evening Tribune.*
*San Diego Union.*
Schantz, Eric Michael. "All Night at the Owl: The Social and Political Relations of Mexicali's Red-Light District, 1913–1925." *On the Border: Society and Culture between the United States and Mexico.* Edited by Andrew Grant Wood. Lanham, MD: SR Books, 2004.

Taylor, Lawrence D. "The Wild Frontier Moves South: U.S. Entrepreneurs and the Growth of Tijuana's Vice Industry, 1908–1955." *Journal of San Diego History* 48 (Summer 2002).

## The Heist on the Dike

Castanien, Pliny. *To Protect and Serve: A History of the San Diego Police Department and Its Chiefs, 1889–1989*. San Diego, CA: San Diego Historical Society, 1993.
*Los Angeles Times.*
*San Diego Evening Tribune.*
*San Diego Sun.*
*San Diego Union.*
Vanderwood, Paul. *Satan's Playground: Mobsters and Movie Stars at America's Greatest Gaming Resort*. Durham, NC: Duke University Press, 2010.

## The Revolutionaries

Camp, Roderic A. *Mexican-Political Biographies, 1935–1993*. Austin: University of Texas Press, 1995.
*Los Angeles Times.*
*New York Times.*
*San Diego Evening Tribune.*
*San Diego Union.*

# DISORDERLY CONDUCT

## A Ruined Woman

*People v. Mayne.* Superior Court case file no. 3812. San Diego, 1889.
*San Diego Sun.*
*San Diego Union.*

# Death of the Butterfly Dancer

*Los Angeles Times.*
*San Diego Evening Tribune.*
*San Diego Sun.*
*San Diego Union.*

# The Royal Coach Affair

Black, Samuel T. *San Diego County, California: A Record of Settlement, Organization, Progress and Achievement.* Chicago: S.J. Clarke, 1913.

Higgins, Shelley. *This Fantastic City, San Diego.* San Diego, CA: City of San Diego, 1956.

*Los Angeles Times.*

*San Diego Union.*

Stone, Harold. *City Manager Government in San Diego.* Chicago: Public Administration Service, 1939.

# The Bribe

Fletcher, Ed. *Memoirs of Ed Fletcher.* San Diego, CA: Pioneer Printers, 1952.

*Los Angeles Times.*

*San Diego Herald.*

*San Diego Union.*

# Dragsters on the Boulevard

Castanien, Pliny. *To Protect and Serve: A History of the San Diego Police Department and Its Chiefs, 1889–1989.* San Diego, CA: San Diego Historical Society, 1993.

Davis, Mike. "Wild Streets: *American Graffiti* Versus the Cold War." *International Socialism Journal* 91 (Summer 2001).

*Los Angeles Times.*

*San Diego Union.*

# FEAR AND INTOLERANCE

## *The Student Strike*

Heilbron, Robert F. "Student Protest at Its Best." *Journal of San Diego History* 20 (Winter 1974).

*Los Angeles Times.*

*San Diego Evening Tribune.*

*San Diego Herald.*

*San Diego Union.*

Wilson, Harlan Leffingwell. "A History of the San Diego City Schools from 1542 to 1942: With Emphasis Upon the Curriculum." Master's thesis, University of Southern California, 1942.

## *The Young Communists*

*Los Angeles Times.*

*San Diego Evening Tribune.*

*San Diego Union.*

Willard, Steve, and Ed LaValle. *San Diego Police: Case Files.* Charleston, SC: Arcadia Publishing, 2012.

## *The Silver Shirts*

Ledeboer, Suzanne G. "The Man Who Would Be Hitler: William Dudley Pelley and the Silver Legion." *California History* 65 (June 1986): 126–36.

*Los Angeles Times.*

*San Diego Union.*

Schwartz, Henry. "The Silver Shirts: Anti-Semitism in San Diego, 1930–1940." *Western States Jewish History* 24 (October 1992): 52–60.

United States Congress. House. Special Committee on Un-American Activities. "Investigation of Nazi Propaganda Activities...." Washington, D.C.: Government Printing Office, 1934.

# A Textbook Controversy

Armstrong, O.K. "Treason in the Textbooks." *American Legion Magazine* (September 1940).

*The Broom.* Special Collections, San Diego Public Library.

Dorn, Charles. "Treason in the Textbooks: Reinterpreting the Harold Rugg Textbook Controversy in the Context of Wartime Schooling." *Paedagogica Historica* 44 (August 2008).

Evans, Ronald W. *The Social Studies Wars: What Should We Teach the Children?* New York: Teachers College, Columbia University, 2004.

———. *This Happened in America: Harold Rugg and the Censure of Social Studies.* Charlotte, NC: Information Age Publishing, 2007.

*Los Angeles Times.*

Rugg, Harold. *That Men May Understand: An American in the Long Armistice.* New York: Doubleday, Doran & Company, 1941.

*San Diego Union.*

*Time.* "Education: Professor Rugg Explains" (April 7, 1941).

# The Last Temptation of the Book Censors

Breed, Clara. *Turning the Pages: San Diego Public Library History, 1882–1982.* San Diego, CA: Friends of the San Diego Public Library, 1983.

Keen, Harold. "Miss Breed's Not for Burning." *San Diego Magazine* (March 1963).

*Los Angeles Times.*

*San Diego Evening Tribune.*

San Diego Public Library. Monthly Reports of the Library Commissioners, March 15, 1963.

*San Diego Union.*

# San Diegans to Remember

## Douglas Gunn

Gunn, Douglas. *Picturesque San Diego: With Historical and Descriptive Notes.* Chicago: Knight & Leonard, 1887.

*An Illustrated History of Southern California: Embracing the Counties of San Diego.* Chicago: Lewis Publishing Company, 1890.

*Los Angeles Times.*

*San Diego Union.*

Smythe, William E. *History of San Diego, 1542–1908.* San Diego, CA: History Company, 1908.

## Albert G. Spalding

Greenwalt, Emmett A. *California Utopia: Point Loma, 1897–1942.* San Diego, CA: Point Loma Publications, 1978.

Levine, Peter. *A.G. Spalding and the Rise of Baseball.* New York: Oxford University Press, 1985.

*New York Times.*

*San Diego Union.*

## Leon de Aryan

*The Broom.* Special Collections, San Diego Public Library.

California Senate. "Report, Joint Fact-Finding Committee on Un-American Activities in California." 55th Sess., 1943.

Cathcart, Ferne. "Heroes of the White Race: C. Leon de Aryan." *CDL Report* 287 (September 2006).

*New York Times.* July 1942.

*San Diego Herald.*

*San Diego Union.*

Steele, Richard W. *Free Speech in the Good War.* New York: St. Martin's Press, 1999.

## Scott O'Dell

Maw, Dolly. "North County Vignettes." *San Diego and Point Magazine* 16 (December 1963).

*New York Times.* October 17, 1989.

Roop, Peter. "Profile: Scott O'Dell," *Language Arts* (November 1984).

Russell, David L. *Scott O'Dell.* New York: Twayne Publishers, 1999.

*San Diego Union.*

*Saturday Evening Review of Literature* (October 30, 1943).

Scott O'Dell. http://scottodell.com.


## Donal Hord

Breed, Clara. *The Library and Donal Hord.* San Diego, CA: San Diego Public Library, 1954.

Ellsburg, Helen. "Donal Hord: Interpreter of the Southwest." *American Art Review* 4 (December 1977).

Hord, Donal. Oral history interview, June 25–30, 1964. Archives of American Art, Smithsonian Institution.

Kamerling, Bruce. "'Like the Ancients': The Art of Donal Hord." *Journal of San Diego History* 31 (Summer 1985).

*San Diego Union.*

# INDEX

# ABOUT THE AUTHOR

R ichard Crawford is the supervisor of Special Collections at the San Diego Public Library. He is the former archives director at the San Diego Historical Society, where he also edited the *Journal of San Diego History*. Born in Long Beach in 1953, he has been a San Diegan since 1973. He has degrees in history (San Diego State University) and library science (San Jose State University). As a historian and archivist, he has written extensively on local history, including articles for the *San Diego Union-Tribune*, as well as in the books *Stranger Than Fiction: Vignettes of San Diego History* (1995) and *The Way We Were in San Diego* (2011).

CPSIA information can be obtained
at www.ICGtesting.com
Printed in the USA
LVOW04*1345160817
545235LV00009B/45/P